VINELAND 1000
by Andrew Sharp

© Andrew Sharp June 1977 Toronto Canada
All Rights Reserved

Andrew Sharp Publications • Toronto

VINELAND 1000

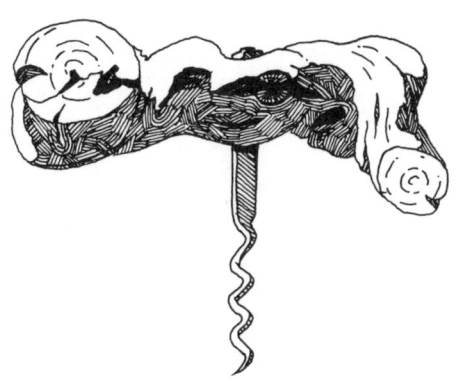

Acknowledgments

A deep debt of gratitude is owed to these individuals. Without their aid VINELAND 1000 would never have become a reality.
In alphabetical order . . .

George Dalgleish
Trudy Gibson
Norman Gilchrist
Suleiman Habib
Donald Mills
Eugene Rosam
Bil & Carol Samotie
Frank Scully
Alfred & Jean Sharp
Robert Sharp
Ernest Spalding
Bob & Irene Thornton

A special debt of gratitude and praise is due my wife, Dayle, not only for her tireless moral support and encouragement but the hundreds of hours spent typesetting, proofing and correcting my many errors. If she knew anything about wine I would have listed her as a co-author. But she doesn't, so I didn't.

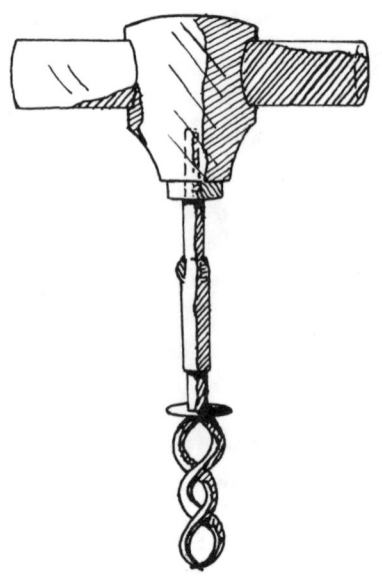

Photographs

1. Bordeaux Cooper   pg. 51
   photo by Bil Samotie

2. Dégorgement   pg. 60
   courtesy Lanson père et fils

3. Candling the wine   pg. 63
   courtesy Bouchard père et fils

4. Wine bottles   pg. 64
   photo by Donald Mills

5. The Winetasters   (top) pg. 69
   courtesy San Francisco Wine Museum

6. A Wine Shop   (bottom) pg. 69
   courtesy San Francisco Wine Museum

7. Corkscrews   pg. 75
   photo by Donald Mills

8. Dr. Fuleki   pg. 101
   courtesy Horticultural Research Station, Vineland, Ont.

9. The Sonoma Valley   (top) pg. 104
   photo by Andrew Sharp

10. Alsace Vineyard   (bottom) pg. 104
    photo by Bil Samotie

11. California Bottling Line   (top) pg. 114
    photo by Andrew Sharp

12. Champagne Bottling Line (bottom) pg. 114
      courtesy Lanson père et fils

13. Burgundy wine pg. 124
      courtesy Bouchard père et fils

14. Champagne cold fermentation tanks (top) pg. 130
      courtesy Lanson père et fils

15. Sebastiani Vineyards of California
      cold fermentation tanks (bottom) pg. 130
      photo by Andrew Sharp

16. Grape harvest in Champagne pg. 132
      courtesy Lanson père et fils

17. Wines of Rome pg. 136
      courtesy San Francisco Wine Museum,
      Christian Bros. Collection

18. Ohio Vineyards (wood engraving) (top) pg. 152
      courtesy San Francisco Wine Museum,
      Christian Bros. Collection

19. California Harvest (wood engraving) (bottom) pg. 152
      courtesy San Francisco Wine Museum,
      Christian Bros. Collection

20. Brandy Still (line engraving) pg. 164
      courtesy San Francisco Wine Museum,
      Christian Bros. Collection

21. Cognac Harvest pg. 166
      courtesy Hennessey Cognac

22. Cognac Distillation pg. 168
      courtesy Hennessey Cognac

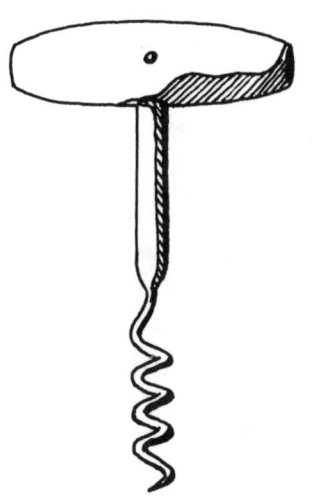

Illustrations

Cover　　　　　　　　　　　　Donald Mills
　　　　　　　　　　　　　　　　Bil Samotie
　　　　　　　　　　　　　　Andrew Sharp

Line Drawings　　　　　　Kevin Thorogood

Contents

INTRODUCTION   7

SECTION I - FROM SMALL BEGINNINGS

Chapter I	- Canadians and the Grape - How We Get Along	11
Chapter II	- Wine Language	18
Chapter III	- The Grapes in Question	24
Chapter IV	- History Books Tell Us	30

SECTION II - QUESTIONS & ANSWERS

Chapter V	- From Grapes to Wine	47
Chapter VI	- How to Treat Wine	65
Chapter VII	- Wine Accessories	71
Chapter VIII	- A Wine Vocabulary	76
Chapter IX	- Wine and Food - The Perfect Partners	81
Chapter X	- Wine and Health	92
Chapter XI	- Canada	99
Chapter XII	- France	113
Chapter XIII	- Italy	134
Chapter XIV	- Germany	143
Chapter XV	- Other Vinelands	149
Chapter XVI	- Wines With a Kick	157

SECTION III - DISTRIBUTION

Chapter XVII	- Controlled Distribution or Free Enterprise?	170
Chapter XVIII	- The Dollars and Cents Of It	183

EPILOGUE   191

Introduction

VINELAND - according to the Viking Sagas, that's what Leif Ericson labelled this land when he first set foot on our shores (circa 1000 A.D.). It was a mistaken identity, of course. Despite the fact that Leif no doubt stumbled across a few wild native vines, VINELAND was a misnomer if there ever was one. Grapes and their noble offspring, wine, were to play about as much a part in Canadian history during the next 900 years as hockey did in Mexico. Yet, despite a rather sluggish start Canada and Canadians may yet lend a ring of truth to Leif Ericson's rather presumptuous comment.

No other country views wine in quite the same manner as Canada. We cast a wary but beckoning eye on this product of the vine. For, we never seem at all certain whether we should embrace it wholeheartedly or lump it together with all the other alcoholic beverages, thought of as socially acceptable **vices.**

If we're ever to get a balanced viewpoint about wine, as Canadians, we must first realize one fundamental reality... the Canadian wine scene today is profoundly divided.

It's invariably catalogued along the lines of, **our** "Domestic" brands compared to, **those** "Imported" wines. Such persistent comparison and competition between these two wine factions has tended to confuse Canadian wine drinkers - forcing many to throw their arms around a cold bottle of beer, in sheer desperation for some straight, unbiased information on the subject.

This schism over wine loyalties is championed on one side by local wine-producers, our grape growers, and their ardent consuming supporters. Formidable opposition is mustered by importers and the supposedly more sophisticated drinkers of "imported" wines. In fact, minor skirmishes and outright wine-warfare is commercially waged on the pages of various stalwarts of the print media and throughout the broadcast industry. The objective of course - more financial followers for their cause.

As wine interest and consumption continues its rapid growth in our land so does wine as a topic of conversation. Taverns, restaurants and associated social gatherings have all become grounds for such discussion, as well as for frequent debate over this domestic vs. foreign issue.

New processing discoveries, promising hybrid varieties of grapes, low priced imports from Communist nations, provincial government support for local wine-producers and grape-growers, plantings of pure European grape varieties . . . all these elements promise to heighten the controversial nature of wine discussions in the future.

In this import vs. domestic squabble (still the heart of the debate), politics, patriotism and price are the most prominent weapons of our local camp; while that foreign opposition makes concerted use of tradition, 'imported' labels, snob appeal and supposed age-old European craftsmanship. To some its become the 'Dandie versus the boy next door' type of scenario.

Sophisticated drinkers of European wines have tut-tutted, nose-in-air, whenever a "domestic" brand was proposed, while once sedate, apple-cheeked little old Canadian grannies have brandished their crystal decanters of Concord wines and assumed threatening poses whenever a "foreign" wine was suggested.

To choose a position between the combatants in this, admittedly civilized conflict may on the surface seem a terribly political stance for any wine writer to take. But this issue has such scarcely perceivable middle ground, the centre posture is not the traditional compromise one might expect.

Nothing short of a sudden disastrous blight of all Canadian vineyards or the introduction of a totally protectionist piece of legislation is going to change the views of either side over this issue. So information from either camp will continue to embody a considerable degree of 'propaganda.' The Canadian consumer must weigh carefully the information presented to him, with respect to its source. Hopefully, in "Vineland 1000" we can assist the consumer in his deliberations and subsequently his choice and appreciation of wines.

When we strip away the bigoted claims and accusations hurled at our native industry and peel off the patriotic veneer coating our domestic offerings we should arrive at something related to a balanced viewpoint . . . a more knowledgeable appreciation of all wines found on the shelves of our Canadian Liquor Control Boards.

Once some basic wine information is taken in medicinal measures it's our ardent desire the Canadian wine-public, you, will simply get more enjoyment out of all honestly made wine. I use the expression "wine-public" instead of wine drinkers in an attempt to include those vastly superior numbers of none-winedrinkers, currently sitting on the sidelines, who will unquestionably join the 'wonderful world of wine' in the near future.

Many of the questions people ask about wine are asked again and again . . . because they're questions we've all asked at one time or another. "Vineland 1000", in Section II, answers directly, 100 of the most asked wine questions - questions Canadian consumers frequently put to the author in his syndicated weekly newspaper column "Wine View." We hope you will enjoy the responses to these questions, not to mention the other two sections of the book, just as much as the odd tipple of the grape.

SECTION I
From Small Beginnings

— Canadians and the Grape — How We Get Along
— Wine Language
— The Grapes in Question
— History Books Tell Us

Chapter I
Canadians & The Grape - How We Get Along

Throughout the ages students of history have voraciously consumed volumes upon volumes of information about the past. Even today there exists growing numbers who are passionately afflicted with the events and costumes of eras long since dead. But almost as old as history itself and consumed in even more prodigious quantities has been the noble product of the vine - WINE.

It too has a long and fascinating story to tell. But alas, it has a reputation that has suffered its ups and downs. One generation had a love affair with it, while another spurned and despised it.

In our modern world, wine is still viewed with varying degrees of respect. To a vast segment of mankind it continues to be taboo. To the opposite extreme, for many, especially in Europe, it's as much a staple as bread. And somewhere in between these two levels of appreciation is found that land so dear to us all, Canada.

Here we find that strange and unique mixture of liberated-conservatism resulting in an attitude towards wine which could only be described as, well . . . different. Good or bad? You'll have to decide for yourselves.

One could imagine the torment of indecision if someone from France was forced to make a singular choice **between** wine or cheese. A similar agony would be evident in someone of Italian extraction if faced with choosing **either** pasta or wine. In each case you would be ill-advised to wager against the wine. But to the vast majority of Canadians, in past generations at least, they wouldn't trade you a broiled hockey puck for a glass of table wine.

Until a very few years ago wine remained for most Canadians, something you bought when you couldn't afford a bottle of rye . . . something you took to that party when it wasn't really worth taking a bottle of the good stuff . . . something a wino splurged on when he was able to scrape up more than the price of rubbing alcohol . . . something at best, Aunt Maudie poured gingerly from the family crystal decanter whenever neighbours dropped in; no one asked for seconds. Yet, attitudes do change and they have for Canadians and wine. After a very long, dry spell we are just beginning to cement a lasting relationship with this most ancient beverage.

Although wine is fast becoming the "in" drink in our land, it has had a rough and extremely exasperating road to travel. The fate of our **native** grapes more often than not, was to be instantly transformed into a jelly, jam or a cheap imitation sherry.

They suffered such inevitable indignities not so much because of enemies, but simply due to a lack of friends. Our North American wine industry, for decades, largely insisted on producing a sweet sticky substance which could be consumed, or should we say sipped, only in limited quantities. This did little in the way of encouraging wine to be an accepted guest at the dinner table.

Governments who already felt their duty was to penalize financially those individuals who drank any alcohol-based beverage, felt it should penalize just a little bit more, those who desired to imbibe anything with an 'off-shore' content. Combine these two attitudes and you produce a society where grape juice outsells wine.

Importers of wine were forced to fight for their very existence with no official recognition, even by Liquor Boards. Yet, much of the credit for the increased appreciation of wine in Canada is due them. Their tenacity has been admirable, even if their motive was more commercial than moral.

Although the government-imposed financial penalties haven't altered, the attitudes in our land have, drastically, almost to a reverse. We say almost because there yet lingers remnants of old prejudices. Evidenced by the fact that many still experience a twinge of conscience every time they pull a cork, as if it were somewhat decadent to drink wine with your meal, sans a suitable special occasion to celebrate.

But facts and figures now mark Canada as one of the world's fastest growing marketplaces for wine. In the past ten years the per capita consumption of wine in our country has grown by more than ninety percent. To get a comparison, during the same period beer consumption grew a mere sixteen percent, while hard liquor gained less than half of that of wine, about thirty-nine percent. But, before you conclude the whole nation is 'hitting the wine bottle', consider that we only down about 1.3 gallons of wine individually per year; while in France and Italy they consume almost thirty gallons per person per year. That could truly be termed 'leaving room for growth.' Reliable forecasts indicate our per capita consumption of wine will quadruple in the next decade.

As well as sheer volume being on the upswing, Canadians have become increasingly sophisticated in their wine tastes. Many have demanded not only the best but variety, too. This has meant the importation of wines from all the famed wine-producing nations in the world. And generally speaking, this is exactly what we have been receiving, the finer vintages these noble vineyards have to offer.

As if these statistics were not sufficient evidence to prove to the most skeptical of minds - that Canada is indeed beginning to take its place in the 'wonderful world of wine' - we have two ultimately undeniable pieces of evidence proving that we have come of age . . . wine-wise. Because we can now unabashedly claim to have in our midst our very own, locally nurtured "wine snobs." Not imported mind you, but home-grown. And something equally as significant but seemingly unique to Canadian culture "anti-wine snobs."

Anti-Wine Snobs

They're unique to Canada in at least one sense. Though most nations view an appreciation of fine wines as at least **one** outward mark of sophistication . . . not so in a number of Canadian social circles. For them an appreciation of wine is a little like a man riding side-saddle.

Precisely how do you define an "anti-wine snob?"

Well, reluctantly we are forced to admit that the Canadian male appears to dominate the role of the "anti-wine" snob. Expressions indigenous to him have almost become Canadian clichés. Whenever he comes face-to-face with a wine drinker he instantly identifies his view of the grape with lines like, "why don't you try something with a little teeth in it?" or, "try one of these, it'll put hair on your chest."

Whenever forced by circumstances to actually purchase a bottle of wine at the liquor store our typical "anti-wine snob" is heard to announce in a whisper that would wake the most seasoned pew-sleeper, "the wine's for the wife you know, never touch the stuff myself!" Never would he purchase a bottle of wine alone. Whether needed or not, his masculine image forces him to include in his order at least three bottles of rye or some other stronger, male associated spirit.

Even before he gets to the cashier this version of the anti-wine snob is easily identified. He's the one who approaches the listing board or stocked shelves with the same pained expression so evident on the faces of husbands whose trip to the drug store included buying sanitary napkins for the wife.

Another version of the "anti-wine snob" appears in a much more subtle fashion. He or she, in this variety, may never come right out and say something against wine. They may even set aside their beer or rye long enough to drink a glass of wine, when some social situation forces them into it - realizing that fashion and society now in Canada have made wine one of the "in" status symbols. If the conversation ever turns to wine even momentarily their classic, self-identifying quip is that cover all bases, never offend anyone, politically endowed expression, "If **YOU** like it, it's a great wine." Heard that somewhere before?

By making light of this whole situation and especially this oft used, sometimes well-meaning expression, we're not trying to indicate that one's personal tastebuds shouldn't be the guiding factor and final arbiter for **what** you drink. Quite the contrary. But wine has been around for a number of centuries. It has and is being drunk by the literal billions of gallons. These two conditions alone have allowed for some international standards to be determined . . . a yardstick by which one can, as objectively as possible view the grape, oblivious to nationalities or personal preferences. Such legitimate standards do exist and connoisseurs of wine throughout the world seem to be in unanimous agreement with them.

So if you were to accept the "anti-wine" snob's premise "it's a great wine, if **YOU** like it" one could and would easily dismiss many of the outstanding wines of the world as inferior and upgrade others not so deserving.

One should never be quite so insecure so as to drink only what the so-called experts say is great, or be so removed from reality to think that just because YOU like it, it must be a great wine. In this instance "like" and "great" are not synonymous.

Experienced wine drinkers often buy and enjoy wines known to be of lesser quality and in some instances even prefer some of these, depending on occasion and accompaniments, to some types that may actually be classified as being of a higher quality. So, personal taste is definitely the master of **which** wines you should drink but it is not always the indicator of which wines are internationally judged as **poor, ordinary, fine** or **great**.

Wine Snob

To this point, if you'll forgive us, we have virtually ignored the anti-wine snob's worthy opposite, the "wine snob." The true wine snob comes in a variety of sizes and shapes; sex discrimination rarely exists in their ranks. Several common habits give clues to their identity, though. A variety well known to many are those who are noticeably uneasy when asked their opinion of a wine, before they've had an opportunity to see the label. Their answer, at this point, could be as cryptic as the Etruscan language. Such individuals are classed as "label" drinkers as opposed to "wine" drinkers.

An even more blatant example of wine snobbery occurs with those who have felt certain social pressures and as a result have economized their efforts in learning about wine. They accomplish this by memorizing the names of a dozen or so of the most famed wines of France. Then begins the name dropping.

They reason, of course, how could one go wrong? Can't one always be socially correct and create the right impression with such distinguished names? After all doesn't a bottle of Chateau Margaux always look good on your table, even if you are at the corner pizzeria?

However small our native group of wine snobs may actually be (Statistics Canada refused to release figures on the actual number) their ranks are being thinned out each year by economics, as the price of very high quality wines continues to skyrocket. If not a disastrous blow to their numbers, the frequency of their appearances should be seriously curtailed.

Then, of course, there appears that rare version of the wine snob who may in fact, actually know something about wine. You come to realize this after the ninth time he's told you so. Always he drinks only the "right" wine with the "right" food and he knows by heart all the so-called rules said to govern this subject. These will be repeated at the slightest excuse. Offer him a peanut and you'll get a dissertation on wine and nuts.

Taken what may be simply acceptable suggestions this version of the wine snob can instantly turn them into hard and fast rules we all must obey if we are ever to establish our standing in the world of wines.

Perhaps forgotten in this case is the fact that no two individual's tastebuds are exactly alike. If you prefer a good Beaujolais with your hot chocolate fudge sundae, who are we to object. It makes you a little weird, but that's your problem.

Only a personal investigation results in the right wine and food affinities for you. Many connoisseurs may legitimately agree about certain food and wine combinations but there are no such hard and fast rules. Explicit suggestions and guidelines are intended more for serving your guests. When you don't know an individual's or a group's personal preferences it's handy to know some combinations that will at least not offend anyone's sensitive palate.

It may take a little time and effort to identify these more acceptable matches, but don't worry. Wine is one of the few subjects where it's more fun to be a slow learner. You just have to keep trying and tasting until you get it right.

Although different in many respects, the wine snob and the anti-wine snob have a good deal in common. For one thing, they succeed in extracting much of the joy from a drink which brings added pleasure to almost any subject or substance. But, happily they more often taint only themselves. As more and more Canadians become knowledgeable about this royalty of beverages both snob and anti-

Chapter I

wine snob will decline and eventually become endangered species.

Having eliminated both snob and anti-wine snob with a few deft strokes of the pen, who do we have left? Aside from you and I of course. Hopefully, we've culled out both extremes and are left with people who are simply interested in knowing more about wine - for the sheer enjoyment of it. Simply stated, to become knowledgeable about wines and to learn to appreciate them, practice makes perfect. No other substitute exists. After all, who would want one?

Many authoritative books are available, along with articles that now appear frequently, even weekly in some areas, in various newspapers across Canada. These can be of great value. For a good deal of satisfaction can be derived by adding to your actual pleasure of drinking wine, the whys and wherefores about the subject.

All too often, national bias is allowed to interfere with true wine appreciation. This nationalistic attitude towards wine (frequently referred to as "grapelism") appears often in Canada but is no stranger in the famed grapelands of France, Italy or Germany either.

The almost universal custom of drinking a glass of wine with one's national flag as a swizzle stick can be dangerous, often resulting in a serious eye injury (a severe case of wine myopia). If Canada has any consolation in this matter it is in the fact that we are preceded in 'grapelism', by virtually all other countries who produce wine. This parochial bigotry for local wine is degrading to wine in general. For wine belongs to man not to countries.

As modest as Canadian wine consumption may seem it would appear we are at last becoming more than just friends with wine. Intimate might be a better choice of adjectives. Not yet a full-blossomed affair, mind you, like that between the French and the grape, but at this rate of growth we could prove to be a suitor of considerable distinction.

The wonderful world of wine is an immense one offering innumerable occasions to experiment and experience. Even the failures are enjoyable. They sharpen the palate for added enjoyment of each success.

Chapter II

Wine Language

Before too many more pages pass by, it becomes essential to establish a few common definitions for several words and phrases that are bound to crop up in this book - like 'wine' for instance. And admittedly, there is some degree of self-protection involved with this exercise.

How often have you found yourself a participant in a heated discussion that finally distilled itself down to the stark realization that you and your opponent simply had quite different definitions for key words to that discussion? Words possess chameleon-like characteristics. Their definitions are subject to various shadings, in direct proportion to the number of users.

To avoid these little misunderstandings that so often end up in large controversies, particular words that form part of a "wine vocabulary" should be defined as succinctly as possible. And what better word to start with than "WINE". For considerably different definitions do exist on respective sides of the Atlantic.

The classic European definition for WINE is stated this way: "wine is the suitable product of the natural fermentation of freshly gathered ripe grapes" - period.

This might appear quite reasonable and logical on first impression. But in North America, the definition of wine is not nearly so precise. On this side of the Atlantic it is, in essence, defined something like this: "wine is made from anything fermentable." Short and sweet

Chapter II

perhaps, but it's enough to curdle the blood of any wine traditionalist.

Blueberries, strawberries, cherries, peaches, blackberries, elderberries, apples, gooseberries, carrots, dandelions, potatoes, honey, tea-leaves and old tennis shoes - all have laid claim to being transformed into wine at some time or another; some commercially, but more frequently by the "home-made" enthusiasts, our basement buffs.

Because of this broadened definition North Americans have seemingly lost some of the critical guidelines by which to judge legitimate wine. And the quality of our native wines has suffered as a bi-product of this philosophy. Personal taste preferences have tended to replace more objective evaluations, as a measure of quality.

Although indisputable as the sole agent for determining what you should drink, personal preferences bear little or no relationship to the quality of the product. On the other side of the coin, those individuals who drink only wines that are considered to be good by the experts, whether they prefer them or not, are just as errant in their approach to the whole subject of wine appreciation. And specifically, neither attitude accomplishes anything favourable for Canadian wines.

In any atmosphere or discipline where loose definitions prevail, standards tend naturally to seek and maintain lower levels. Inferior quality becomes excusable as personal taste. Local oddities become patriotic symbols to be defended as ardently as one would motherhood.

The basic chemical reaction involved with fermentation is Sugar + Yeast = Alcohol + Carbon Dioxide. Mix this with any flavouring agent and you will yield an alcoholic beverage of a sort. But does it have the right to be labelled wine?

Grapes, in this writer's view, have a traditional right to the exclusive use of the term 'wine'; a tradition extending back into history over 4,000 years, from Babylon, to Egypt, to Assyria, to Persia, to Greece, to Rome, to France and finally on to this "new world" - an unbroken historical chain.

All the necessary ingredients to accomplish the transformation from fresh grapes to wine are naturally present within the grape itself. Natural yeast spores are present by the millions on the outside of the grape skin. When crushed they begin to react with the natural sugars within the grape. This reaction continues until a natural level of eight to fourteen percent of alcohol is created - then the reaction halts. The yeast cells can only put up with so much alcohol, like most of us, and when this natural level is achieved, its self-regulatory controls stop further alcohol production.

By this time, essentially all the natural grape sugars have been consumed and a very dry wine results. Yes, that's right! The natural offspring of squeezing fresh grapes and letting them take their natural course, is a dry wine and not a sweet grape juice, as some factions of our society would have us believe. Chemicals must be added to squeezed grapes to stop them from doing what comes naturally, turning into wine.

If you don't already know or haven't at this point guessed, the definition of the term 'dry' as it applies to wine, refers to its sugar content. A 'dry' wine is one with little or no sweetness; not a shortage of water. And it certainly does not refer to that unquenchable thirst associated with the morning after an evening spent, shall we say, immoderately.

Our description here of how grapes turn into wine is a gross generalization, to be remedied in following chapters. Despite the fact an alcoholic liquid can be made from a variety of substances, there is serious challenge to it all being defined as wine. And this, even though some countries concede that labels for such products precede the word WINE with the name of the fruit used, such as PEACH wine or BLUEBERRY wine, etc.

Common to virtually all other fruits or vegetables which are made into a so-called wine is the need to add either sugar, yeast or water. Usually all three are necessary to start and complete the reaction economically. Although on rare occasions judicious quantities of these ingredients are added to grapes by their producers, it is usually done to improve or alter the reaction in some way; to achieve a specific goal or type of wine. It is never mandatory to form an economical reaction in the first place.

Sugar, yeast and water are naturally present in grapes to an optimum degree when compared to other fruits. No other fruit possesses the needed levels of these ingredients to produce such prodigious quantities of wine. This will explain why from the world's vineyards flows a vintage of nearly seven billion gallons of GRAPE wine annually.

If you were to combine all these **mock** wines, made from every other fruit, their annual vintage wouldn't yield enough liquid to dampen all the corks used in grape-wine production. From the vineyard, to the bottle, to you, fermented grapes should retain the sole privilege to be known as WINE.

Wine, vin, vino, wein or however you choose to express it, it deserves universal recognition and definition. After all, what else is communication all about, but to share a mutual understanding. To make room for some local fruit or vegetable beverage to be defined as wine simply detracts from this goal. And it unnecessarily infringes on the exclusivity of fermented grapes to be known as wine; authorized by thousands of years of tradition and billions upon billions of gallons of production.

This is in no way intended to slight beverages made from other fruits. They can be very palatable, some quite delicious. But in our view, they are not wine! Call them what you will, anything but wine.

Indeed, honest producers should be proud to give the fruits of their labour a distinctive, a unique identification. Distilled grape-wine could never be called Whiskey, nor would its producers ever desire to make such a pretense. They are justly proud of their very private designation, Brandy (or Cognac, depending on its place of origin).

This may or may not have been a convincing argument. But for all intents and purposes, whenever reference to "WINE" is made in these pages, we do so to the offspring of a grape and to no other fruit. Even if you haven't been totally converted, if you promise not to look for any consideration of apple or blueberry wines, we'll promise not to pass on any recipes for grape cookies.

Despite local interpretations wine language through individual word and expression is quite exacting as are most other legitimate fields of endeavour. Words such as GREAT, FINE, ORDINARY and POOR find less room each year for personal interpretation, when describing wines.

When we use the word "GREAT" in reference to a wine's overall quality, we are discussing the elite of the wine world. We are describing a wine that is virtual perfection, ideally balanced in all of its attributes. Perfect body, aroma, bouquet, acidity, texture, finish, and a dozen other attributes a "great" wine must exemplify. Far less than one percent of all the wine in the world will ever achieve this pinnacle.

"Fine" is a favourite term of advertisers when describing their clients' wares, especially if it's wine. It's also the most misapplied adjective in many wine vocabularies. Although "fine" is somewhat more flexible in its application, nevertheless, FINE WINES must be outstanding wines. The slightest flaw might be forgivable. But any further shortcomings would be inexcusable. Certainly less than five percent of each year's world production will be able to legitimately stand on this plateau.

At best, over ninety percent of the world's wines will achieve a distinction rated no higher than "ORDINARY." 'Vin ordinaire' is truly the wine most familiar to the vast majority of winelovers. It is common everyday table wine to be consumed with, at most, passing interest in its parentage. But an "ordinary" wine, is still deserving of compliments. It represents genuine praise for its vintners and indeed, many wines often thought of as 'noble' are firmly entrenched in this category.

Assessing your host's wine as being on the "POOR" side should not be considered an insult to him. Whether or not you wish to tell him that face to face will vary from host to host. Poor wines are not the best example of the enologist's art but they're quite drinkable. They are non-descript wines; could originate from anywhere in the world and will most frequently be impossible to define in terms of grape parentage. But they are palatable and can be enjoyed best with a meal.

It's in one's self-interest to have these definitions well in mind and at the ready for any occasion whereupon your host may ask you, how you enjoyed a particular wine. And remember, it's probably his favourite he's asking about. So before putting your foot into his wine glass, it's not unwise to pre-condition him with some common terminology.

If it perchance should be a 'great' or even a 'fine' wine it should be quite simple to avoid any strain on your friendship. But if you must label his wine 'ordinary' defining what that really means in wine language might be soothing to the situation. And if your conscience dictates the decision 'poor', well . . . you'll just have to

Chapter II

evaluate your ability to outrun a wine bottle launched by an irate former friend. Or else, make doubly sure he knows what you're talking about when you make such quality judgments.

However, if a long inborn streak of cowardice runs through your family, in such matters, and you'd prefer not to be quite so frank, you can always fall back on an old standby, "nice". It is a truly meaningless word when applied to wine. And I for one, have consumed my fair share of **nice** wines in my time.

Within these four divisions, great, fine, ordinary and poor there are undoubtedly scores of intermediate graduations. In fact some experts choose to put another complete classification, that of "NOBLE", between 'fine' and 'ordinary'. The number of such categories varies according to how broad or definitive the wine writer may choose to be, to suit his purpose at the moment. We'll settle for four on this occasion. But as one rather earthy connoisseur once phrased it - "there are only two classes of wine . . . drinkable and undrinkable." It seems to say it all.

There are numerous other 'wine words' and expressions in need of definition but to avoid turning this into a dictionary we'll treat such words as we meet them.

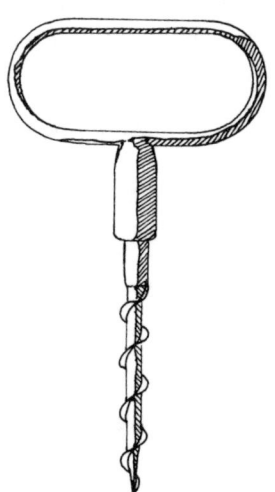

Chapter III

The Grapes in Question

Inextricably involved in any consideration of Canadian wines compared to Imported wines are the two very distinctly different grape families or species from which these wines originate.

Labrusca

The most prominent native Canadian grape family is named Vitis Labrusca. Although there are other families used in vinting Canadian wines, they are so similar in character and, by comparison are used in such small quantities, we need not go into any further descriptions.

A slang expression often used to describe Vitis Labrusca is "FOX" grape. Although usage of this expression far from pleases some notable individuals in the Canadian Wine Industry, we find it a descriptive and legitimate expression for continued use.

This term 'foxy' is used to denote the very potent, pungent, grapey taste and aroma, characteristic of the Labrusca species of grapes. "Slip-skin" is another colloquial expression frequently employed to describe how easily the pulp of the Labrusca grape is separated from its skin. I can remember as a youngster picking wild Labrusca grapes in Southwestern Ontario, outside the small village of Watford. It became a fine art to pinch a single grape and have the flying pulp accurately hit the target you were aiming at - targets like an open mouth, the back of a passing head or someone else's open mouth.

Chapter III

Other notable qualities common to this species of grape are its relatively low sugar content and high acid levels. These two factors have increased significance when held in the light of one of the most common slurs cast upon Canadian wines.

Canadian wineries are frequently charged with using too much sugar (chaptalisation) and adding too much water to stretch the gallonage of their wines. This is generally regarded as a **no-no** in the wine industry.

The traditionally low sugar content of Labrusca grapes grown in our Northern climate legitimately calls for some sugar to be added during the wine-making process, to produce the required level of alcohol. This very same practice is no stranger to the northern vineyards of Germany either. The only difference when German vintners use sugar during those vintages that require sugar are the complaints they don't get as a result.

The objective of adding cane-sugar to any dry table wine during fermentation is not to sweeten it, but to increase the alcohol level achieved during processing. But when a producer chooses to use sugar to increase the end sweetness of the wine, as in the production of some cheap sherry-type wines, objections to this practice are justified. In time hopefully pride in product will totally eliminate these already diminishing examples of "fabricated" wines.

The basis for public stone-throwing over water that is allegedly used to stretch Canadian wines is, how utterly destructive such a practice would be if used with European vinifera grapes. The subtle flavours of vinifera grapes with their lower acid levels cannot stand being stretched. The flavour of these wines and their tartness would be seriously affected. As well, the wine would be subject to early spoilage because of the diluted acid levels (acid being a natural preservative in wines).

But the same is not true for the wines made from our North American Labrusca species. As we have already mentioned their flavour compounds are extremely potent and the Labrusca species, in our climate, tends to higher acid levels. This means flavour-wise, they most assuredly can stand to be stretched, and indeed some expert opinions express the feeling that this is better for them. Labrusca wines, even when stretched, reserve sufficient acid to preserve the wine and hold an agreeable degree of tartness.

Legislation does however, realistically set two hundred and twenty-five gallons of wine per ton of grapes as a maximum for Canadian wines. And although such a practice will never result in fine wines, it is not illegitimate when your height of expectation is "vin ordinaire".

In contrast to this practice of sugaring (chaptalisation), some wine producing areas such as California actually have state legislation which outlaws the addition of any sugar to their wines. The local vintners tout this almost as a symbol or act of wine chastity or purity. But, they parade this banner a little too proudly. Because for areas such as California to pass legislation outlawing the addition of sugar would be similar to legislating that you can't add water to a watermelon. Who needs it?

In such areas, where the sun generally predominates to the degree it does in California (there are micro-areas that don't get as many sun hours), the grape naturally produces all the sugar it needs, and then some.

In 1971 new laws were enacted in Germany which in effect divided all German wines into one of three general classifications, 'Tafelwein', 'Qualitatswein' and 'Qualitatswein Mit Pradikat'. All but the last designation, Quality Wines of Distinction, are permitted to have sugar added, when necessary.

The types of wine which come under this latter German classification are produced from grapes that are allowed to remain on the vine for prolonged lengths of time, until they are very ripe, and are high in natural sugar content. So, again some of this legislation does tend towards being of the watermelon class, or at least has that affect in application.

Vinifera

On the opposite side of our grape comparison chart is the species of grapes known as "VITIS VINIFERA" - commonly called the "wine bearer". This is the species found in all European vineyards and indeed in all vineyards of the world with the exception of those in Canada and the Eastern United States. Californian wines originate almost exclusively from the Vinifera family; originally transplanted from Europe.

Vinifera is the species of grape that has been cultivated from the beginning of recorded wine history, some 4,000 years ago. All of the truly great and fine wines of the world come from this species.

It produces at its best, a wine of subtle bouquet and aroma. When 'great' its taste is luscious, fruity, well-balanced in all its attributes, never overbearing.

As glorious as this may sound, never to be forgotten is the fact that this same Vinifera grape family, fathers millions upon millions of gallons of the most horrendous liquid ever to be sold for human consumption. And it performs this act each and every year. "Plonk" is one of the kinder terms associated with these disasters.

If you've ever witnessed a bulk tanker in a European port being pumped full of hundreds of thousands of gallons of wine you begin to appreciate how ordinary, ordinary can get. Enough is usually spilled over into the harbour to perk up Charlie Tuna's day.

We might consolingly add for all those other vineyard nations that much of this "plonk" emanates from France itself. It's difficult to comprehend, and for some wine bigots impossible to accept, that as well as producing more 'great' wines than all other lands combined, France sinks to the dregs of the barrel with the worst of them.

Never to be overlooked though, is that vinifera varieties continue to set the world standard for wine-producing grapes. To ignore this dictum and insist that any other species is capable of achieving such heights is to live in a world of commercial dreams. In fact holding to such a viewpoint would seriously hinder those lands from ever achieving their full wine potential.

In both Ontario and British Columbia vineyard regions, very small quantities of pure vinifera varieties are now being cultivated. The Gamay, the Riesling, Chardonnay and Pinot Noir, all famous European grape varieties, are trickling to market. But with a difference. They're sporting 'Made in Canada' labels.

So, to produce everyday drinking wines, vin ordinaires, using native Labruscas and their hybrids is truly a realistic goal for Canadian wine producers. It's an accessible goal and to some degree it's been achieved already.

When legislation introduced first by the Ontario government - reducing its profit margins on Ontario wines (from 67% to 37% on table wines), allowing the blending of bulk imported wines and the importation of fresh grapes and concentrates - is implemented, followed certainly by other provinces, Canadian wines, or a blend of them at least, will become increasingly attractive from all aspects. We may yet have a genuine vin ordinaire with a vin ordinaire price tag.

Hybrids

Hybrids or crossbreeds are looked to and generally have a history of improving the harvest in many areas of agriculture. And to a limited degree grape hybrids can be included in this statement.

The objective of a hybrid is to breed an offspring with a specific set of characteristics more adaptable and desirable for an established set of circumstances. This very objective is the motivating factor behind such research in the Canadian programme of grape hybridizing.

Our Canadian climate and soil conditions demand that if a species of grape is going to survive here and produce economically it must be hardy, prolific and highly disease resistant. Our native Labrusca more than fills the bill in this respect.

But alas, the distinctive taste and aroma it imparts to its wine is becoming less and less acceptable to the general Canadian wine public. The more subtle qualities of the imported European vinifera wines are filling this shifting demand in the manner of soaring imported wine sales.

This switch from the more prominent, stronger tasting beverages to ones of a lighter nature is evident in other areas of alcohol consumption, too. Lighter Scotches are experiencing an upswing in sales, as are white rums when compared to dark rums. Vodka sales are on the rise as well. These gains in market share pinpoint the definite change from the heavier more traditional drinks to those of lighter character. This precludes of course, our seemingly never ending preference for rye whisky.

An obvious reaction to this very Canadian grape problem might seem to be · simply cultivate and vint wines from transplanted European viniferas. However, that's tantamount to saying, just build a rocket and send it to the moon. For viniferas just aren't passionately in love with our local climate, don't proliferate as well here as our Labruscas, and aren't as disease resistant. Add all this up and you can see why it's easier to build that rocket. Ah, ha! Crossbreeds you say, right?

That is one solution and some thirty years ago a programme to develop hybrid grapes from which one might mix and extract the most appropriate qualities was undertaken here.

Some very interesting and encouraging results have come to light in the past few years. Results that could be called a ray of sunshine for the Canadian wine industry, not a full-fledged sunburst, mind you, but nevertheless, definitely a ray.

Certain varieties of these hybrids have been chosen for use in major commercial production and are now becoming available in sufficient quantities for mass release to the public, unblended with any native Labrusca varieties. Things are looking up for our locals. Names like Marechal Foch, de Chaunac, Chelois, Verdelet, Villard Noir and Veeburg are names that are bound to become an increasing part of a Canadian wine vocabulary. Despite the fact that most of these hybrids were developed in Europe the important factor is that they were bred for hardy climates and they have taken to the Canadian vineyards like a beaver to water.

What remains to be seen is the effect of Ontario's loosening its restrictions on its home wineries and their importing of bulk wines, fresh grapes and concentrates. Will it stimulate the prophesied growth in sales for Canadian wineries or will it simply result in an apathy settling upon local grape growers? Will they continue to exchange the grape varieties in their vineyards, from pure Labrusca to superior hybrids and viniferas? Or will they be simply content to supply what they have now for blending with the imported raw materials? To know for certain you'd have to be a true prophet. But if we were to go by past experience - self improvement by our industry will probably slow to a slower snail's pace.

Chapter IV

History Books Tell Us

Right from the beginning opinions concerning Canadian wines were extremely diverse. If you were to listen to or read just one side of the issue, the domestic, you might feel a new wine Nirvana had been discovered in Canadian vineyards. Or contrastingly, if you paid much attention to the critics, you might be convinced that grapes had no future whatsoever in our land.

North American grape history opened up first around the year 1000 A.D. when according to the Viking sagas Leif Ericson first set sail and planted a fur-clad foot on the soil of a new hemisphere. He obviously ran across a few wild grapes, as the report goes, enough to cause him to name this new world Vineland, a misnomer if there ever was one.

We can skip past a few hundred years, for the next historical reference to the grapes of North America came early in the 1600's when Captain John Smith, of Pocahontas fame, recorded the discovery of prodigious quantities of native vines in the area of the Virginia Colony. He stated at the time they were: "Fatte grapes with juice thicke" but added: "the taste doth not so well please when made into wine."

It appears John hadn't wasted much time before trying to whip up a local concoction, but he definitely wasn't too thrilled with the initial results. Whether it was his skill as a winemaker, or the quality of the grapes which so soured him, we'll never know.

Chapter IV

But now, compare John Smith's findings with that of some Jesuit priests in Quebec just a few years later. In "La Jeune's Relations" of 1636, they stated: "In some places there are many wild vines loaded with grapes; some have made wine of them through curiosity; I tasted it and it seemed to me very good."

Immediately you can see the issue blooms into a controversy of considerable proportion. Trying to decipher wherein the truth lies, just between these two early, unrelated, yet opposing statements, seems an impossible task from this vantage point in history.

Yet, some might quickly demand, who are you going to believe, a priest or a well known seventeenth century gad-about such as old John? Depending upon your personal persuasion, the answer might seem blatantly obvious.

However, setting aside the traditional feelings towards those in clerical habits, the other view might rightly inquire, who would probably have the greater experience and subsequently the more educated palate to be able to make such lofty taste assessments - a man of the world or someone whose extra-curricular activities have been curtailed by a celibate marriage to an institution. For them the right answer also might seem quite obvious.

Again though, the pro side might quickly remind us of the notable record different orders of the church have achieved in the development of wine, liqueurs and even some wine-based jams and jellies. Of course, this might illicit the retort that whenever one divides their interests too radically, neither endeavour is crowned with much success! And so on and on might go these offerings of 'for instances' and 'what abouts' without any final resolution ever being reached.

However, it must seem somewhat obvious even to the most casual spectator, the views concerning the quality of our early North American wines were divergent. And it would be impossible for us to determine if the length of time between these early pioneers' last taste of the wines of their homeland and their first introduction to these new native vintages was long enough to dull that sense of taste appreciation.

John Smith's opinion seemed to prevail in his neighbourhood for shortly thereafter, in 1616, Lord Delaware arranged for the transplanting of European vines to North American shores along with the skilled help needed to nurture and tend them.

Neither the vines nor the personnel did well and the whole experiment proved a monumental failure. Closely following this in 1629, more vines and viticulturalists were imported from Europe for another valiant effort. Their fate proved no finer.

One more major attempt to cultivate viniferas in North America was tried on Rhode Island, before it seemed apparent that, wine-wise, our "foxy" native Labrusca simply had to be faced.

Canadian history went silent on grapes for the next two hundred years or so, and in 1811 came the first recorded reference to wines since 1636.

At this time a German Army Corporal, one Johann Schiller, who had settled in Cooksville, was making and selling the odd jug of wine. It was vinted strictly from the wild Labruscas growing in the area. Today, Schiller is labelled the "father of Canadian Winemakers." And by 1860 there were already a number of other German farmers making their own wines; most likely of a sweeter dessert variety rather than dry table wines, which had yet to come into vogue.

But the first individual thought to actually plant and cultivate vines locally was a man named Porter Adams around 1857. From the 1860's onward, the idea seemed to catch on in a commercial way. Wineries began to take root in various communities across south-western Ontario and by 1864 even a Canadian Vinegrowers association had been formed.

Between 1860 and 1900 the controversy over the best type of grape for use in commercial production was being hotly disputed among the local growers. Some vehemently rejected and condemned Concords, praising such varieties as the Delaware. Others felt the Concord's productivity made it the most suitable grape for commercial usage. Already business and good taste were at odds.

By 1868 the major crops were Concord, Delaware, Clinton, Diana and Isabella; selling for four to five cents a pound. Later the highly prolific and hardy Concord, even though it was one of the poorer wine grapes, won out in its bid to dominate Canadian vineyards. Only in recent years is it beginning to significantly yield its grip, due to concerted consumer demands.

Such a veritable babe to the world of wines, as Canadian wineries were, they had much to overcome in the way of criticism and indiscriminate slurs that were cast upon their future potential. Because of this an understandable sensitivity developed in our domestic industry causing it at times to grasp at the proverbial straw where compliments were concerned. Awards of questionable significance were too often hailed as major achievements and still are.

The ease with which those who are biased towards Canadian wines accept supposed international compliments is of concern today. It merits serious re-assessment as such false, undeserved pride does little to encourage the continual upgrading our domestic product so dearly needs. If this attitude persists, in its present form, it could well lull us into a feeling we have international acclaim, which in truth we yet neither merit nor possess.

It's somewhat perplexing, as well, when you realize that too often those who today are responsible for formulating the marketing and public relations approaches for Canadian wineries have little in the way of a wine background, and thus little affinity for wine at all. They may have been excellent people in their field but again, too often that field, even though it may have been in marketing and sales, was with non-related consumer products.

They then mistakenly try to market wine like a shaving lotion or some other toiletry. A goodly proportion of Canada's wine industry is controlled by larger corporations who have made their mark with other alcoholic beverages. Efforts to sell their wine brands like their beer or whisky labels hasn't met with success. In all likelihood it never will. Unless these corporations make some radical changes and approach the consumer with their wine wares in a much altered fashion native wines will continue to lose a larger and larger share of total sales in Canada.

The scapegoat for their failure to sell as much Canadian wine as they should turns out to be those nasty "imported" wines again. Blaming low cost imports for all their woes gains them some sympathy from certain consumers and official sources but in reality it focuses attention in the wrong direction. A direction in which they will not find the solution to their many problems. Even complaints that other lands subsidize their wine industry, therefore making it tough for them to compete is not quite as accurate as it sounds and again avoids the issue of a management without an affinity for wine.

Another complaint, more in the nature of a whining, that sadly appears to be getting a listening ear from government agencies concerns the number of Liquor Board listings allotted to 'Imported' wines. Canadian producers persist in their shouts of 'foul' over the 60-40 split - favouring Imported brands - they get on the listing boards.

On the surface it might seem a little unfair that our own Domestic labels have the smaller 40% share. But how quickly matters are brought into perspective when we realize that France alone annually loses, to evaporation, several times as much wine as Canada produces each year. The same is true for each Italian vintage. Our Canadian vintage actually represents less than one fifth of 1 percent of all the wine vinted annually. We protest too loudly, methinks.

These statistics are even more significant when we consider that if every Canadian wine drinker turned to buying only Canadian, almost half of the wine drinkers in our country would have to go without. The simple fact of the matter is - Canadian wineries cannot now produce sufficient wine, without importing grapes or concentrates, to supply the current demand for wine in our nation.

Canadian producers have too many labels for their own good. Each small winery takes an unhealthy shotgun approach to marketing. They try vainly to reproduce every variety of wine made . . . hoping upon hope one label will find extraordinary consumer acceptance and pay the public relations and advertising bills for the others. Such diversity of labels is not really in the best interest of our Domestic industry.

Canadian producers of wine are faced with two momentous stumbling blocks to their continued progress and market gains . . . the problem of growing (not buying and importing them) the right grapes from which to make their wine and the failure to realize that you need the right people, with a fine appreciation for and an extensive knowledge about wine. You need both to build a clientele that will support you over the long term.

Yet shortages of both continue to inhibit our domestic industry. Government subsidies will not correct these fundamental faults.

Prohibition

As World War I approached its mid point (1916) it marked for the

Chapter IV

Canadian wine industry the beginning of its most disastrous era. The approaching 10 year period (actually 10 years, 8 months, 2 weeks, 1 day and 15 hours) was to set wine and the Canadian wine industry back fifty years.

As yet the valleys of British Columbia had not been introduced to the grape in a significant way. To this point in Canadian grape history southwestern Ontario remained the only wine producing region in our nation.

Consumption of alcohol was beginning to fall on hard times. It had become a public scapegoat for virtually every social ill. And at length a "temperance" attitude, supported by the United Farmers' Party, had somehow gained a strangle-hold on the Ontario provincial legislature. Its motivating force, the various so-called Christian temperance movements, were quick to see that demon rum, and all its sinful cohorts, wine included, were placed on the forbidden list, and were indeed legally strangled. Prohibition had cast its insidious shadow on another land. (The U.S. falling as well).

But alas, as with so many other placard-carrying, vociferous take-to-the-street movements, who mind you, have nothing but our best interests at heart, they managed to make things worse than before. The majority of the Canadian populace, despite the fact they still wanted to tipple their favourite libation, meekly abrogated this right to the will of the more volatile, organized minority - a habit that was to grow more popular as the next few decades passed.

After all, who ever heard of organizing drinkers? It may be quite all right to tip the odd glass and even share a dram or so with your friends, but an out and out drinkers organization - never! The majority was to forever remain silent on this matter. So the more militant, organized temperance groups did prevail - for a while at least.

At least, until a few grape-growers realized you can only make so much jam and jelly out of all those tons of grapes. They complained loudly about their wine being included on this banned beverage list. In fact their complaints were so loud they echoed about the halls of Queen's Park until its provincial legislators were forced to drop wine from the infamous list, just to stop the ringing in their ears. The dollar had gained another small victory, where reason couldn't.

The temperance and prohibitionist influence wasn't to take this sitting down. After all they hadn't marched all this way to be beaten by a grape and a few of its friends. Even though wine was now the only legal alcoholic beverage (you needed a doctor's prescription to get any spirits) a new curve was thrown at this youthful industry. Again, only for our own good, the temperance government enacted legislation making it mandatory that each purchase of wine be in minimum lots of one five gallon keg or one twelve bottle case. That went a long way to promote temperance, as anyone could plainly see. Of course, their purpose was to make each purchase large enough to be financially discouraging. Someone surely felt **sin** was the sole privilege of the wealthy. Anyway . . .

As if this wasn't already enough "good" to do to wine drinkers; they were going to have to travel further to get their allotment. For each winery was allowed to sell its products only from one outlet and that to be attached to the winery. And as cars weren't quite so plentiful in those days, it was a major undertaking, for those thirsty enough to make the sojourn from other Ontario centres to the Niagara region. They were lucky to make it back home with anything left in the jug.

Because of these restrictions, where outlets were concerned, some producers, now so remote from their markets felt forced to move their wineries to larger population centres, consequently further and further away from the vineyards. This explains why today you still find wineries in such unlikely cities as London and Toronto. Neither of their surrounding territories grow grapes, yet they do have one vital ingredient needed to keep any wine business liquid - paying customers with a thirst.

The grape-growers exerted enough pressure in the right places to make certain there were enough outlets, in the form of wineries, to use up their growing grape crops. In an attempt to keep these grape-growers placated the Board of Liquor Commissioners were prone to dole out licenses rather freely, might we say. In the ten year period of prohibition alone, more than thirty new wineries were licensed by the Province.

Wineries in name only, for many were not much more than a back room with a bathtub in which to vint their wares. As there were few regulations and fewer inspections, little could be done to control such operations. Often they were in the back room of a grocery store and sold liberally with the weekly grocery order. Or for those wrestling with their conscience, they were bottled and sold as various tonics and medicines.

The thirst for alcoholic beverages both in Canada and below the border, the lack of controls and conscience, all fostered and encouraged by the atmosphere prohibition created, sent the quality level of Canadian wines, and thusly appreciation for wine in general, for a nosedive - straight down. With few exceptions our Canadian wine industry was fully deserving of all the crude and derogatory remarks heaped upon it. Rotgut, swill, squreech were some of the kinder terms used to describe the wines emanating from some of these producers.

Prohibition had created a thirst that had, to a large degree, destroyed any sense of good taste. The huge sponge-like market to the south of the border, where even native wineries had been outlawed, soaked up a considerable portion of Canadian production (illegally of course). And our American friends, long-suffering from this social drought weren't looking for Chateau-bottled Bordeaux either. Their standards demanded little in the way of quality and a number of our international bootlegging producers weren't about to provide any - only quantity.

But several problems faced these opportunist wineries. Some grape growers succumbed to persistent temperance pressure and refused to sell their grapes for wine production. This pushed up the price of even poor crops - prices of $100 to $120 per ton were not uncommon. And this for inferior crops of Concord; even inferior where Concord crops were concerned. Such prices were not to be paid again till the inflated seventies arrived. And strangely enough Concords were still to abound.

To solve the problem of raw material shortage and to supply the level of product demand an old standby was re-introduced to the local wine trade - water. Now here's a noble substance - long respected - well known in the ice cube trade - a firm supporter of the national game of hockey - why not. After all they wouldn't be the only wine industry in the world who **cut** the grape with a few thousand gallons of water. It became now unknown for some to get up to 600 gallons of wine out of every ton of grapes. It's probably well that modern refrigerators were a few years off, for with that percentage of water, such colder temperatures would have turned most of these offerings into wine-flavoured popsicles, with very little exposure.

And yet another problem arose for these producers. Once stretched to such degrees it was difficult to produce the realistic red colour red wines are supposed to have. And as red wines were nearly 5 times as popular as whites this presented a major hurdle.

Without the modern, safe, vegetable dyes commonly used today to give products that "natural" look, these unscrupulous producers turned to using coal tar dyes and other even more formidable additives to doctor up respectable wine-like tints. This 'colouring' practice, unforgivable in those circumstances, however, continues with us today in more legitimate and considerably safer ways.

And here you thought that those glorious golden hues in your 12-year-old bottle of Scotch came from years of tender ageing in oaken casks. One thing modern Scotch Whisky, Rye Whisky, Bourbon and Brandy have in common is the caramel-based additive used to give them those glorious shades. Is there nothing sacred anymore?

Yet, today because of restricted yields of wine per ton of grapes, colouring of wine is non-existent in any wine-producing nation. Especially is this true for Canadian wines. Government controls and inspection make such liberties essentially impossible.

To avoid blanket accusations it's imperative we mention not all Canadian wineries of this **dry** era engaged in these shoddy practices. Some of the producers remained reliable, trustworthy wine-makers. Perhaps certain standards may have had a tendency to relax somewhat, but on their part there was no wholesale abandonment of conscience towards their products.

By the late 1920's the steam behind the prohibition movement had begun to wane. The public, perhaps from simply tiring of the clandestine actions and contortions they had to go through to hide their drinking habits, made their temperment known to those in authority - who were also tired of drinking their beer from teacups.

The Tory party led by Howard Ferguson defeated the prohibitionist United Farmers' party on a straight Liquor Control platform. Eventually the whole land was to restore to the imbiber some degree of respectability.

Chapter IV

Yet there was no drunken revolt or uprising to mark the death of prohibition in 1927. It quietly slipped into oblivion to join that great wasteland of other disagreeable government policies past, present and in years to come.

Even dyed-in-the-wool abstainers had to admit, the bootleggers, the criminal influence, the phony prescriptions, the poor product, the suspicious attitudes and the smuggling encouraged by Prohibition was doing little to accomplish worthwhile social attitudes.

The new government's attitude, firmly set against a total forbidding of alcohol, became one of strict governmental "control". And by the late 1920's most provinces had passed a Liquor Control Act . . . embarking on a program of legislating and control of alcoholic drinks.

Despite continual and progressive relaxing of some of these earlier controls, it would be nearly 50 years before these agencies began to publicly acknowledge that such control must in the end, resort to the individual . . . he truly must be his own "Liquor Control Board."

Post Prohibition

Prohibition was over. But what a long road back for Canadian wine producers. Their reputation, if you could refer to it as a reputation, had bottomed out. It could get no worse. The only course left open, as the proverbial saying goes, was up. But how quickly could it recover, if at all? Monumental questions indeed.

While under the burden of prohibition each winery that was licensed by the former Board of Liquor Commissioners was allowed one retail outlet for its products. Up until the end of prohibition and the establishment of the new Liquor Control Board, 51 licenses had been issued in Ontario, still the only province with a wine industry of any significance.

And so it was decided, that aside from government operated stores only 51 private retail stores, one for each licencee, could be operated by these Ontario wineries. No additional private outlets would be permitted for almost 50 years. By that time (late 1976 early 1977) it had become, for most wineries, an economic uncertainty as to whether they could even afford to operate their current number of stores, let alone add new outlets.

To some, the coming years meant the new Board and the wineries set about the noble task of upgrading their products and our native wine industry as a whole. This was only a polite way of expressing optimistic conjecture. For, the public had more to say about this than given credit for. More than a noble goal it was simply - upgrade or die. If you ever hoped to market wine in a land of traditional spirit and beer drinkers, it was an absolute necessity to have a quality product.

The liquor board and private outlets were now open and in high gear for the expected flood of business. But the wine was no more ready or drinkable than it was during those disastrous dry years.

During prohibition wine was basically all that could be bought, in the way of adult-type beverages. As bad as that wine was there was little point in complaining - you paid your money and kept quiet. But now since many government agencies had stuck their fingers into the pie, for their share of the expected wealth, their **was** somebody to which complaints could be directed. And complain the public did.

They complained where it's heard best, in the pocketbook. The protests flooded into the new Board like the tide on the Bay of Fundy. Too vinegary - too much sediment - bottles exploding from second fermentations - too much sugar - too many chemicals - not enough grapes - too much water - foreign matter in the bottles - dirty bottles - strange tasting, and a plethora of other complaints were lodged with the board.

Our new Board leaped into action with what was to become its trademark rate of movement - akin to a cautious snail with a broken leg. Yet, in all fairness to the Board, there was little in the way of guidelines. And each movement was as if breaking new sod. The debate continues today as to whether the Liquor Boards are one generation behind public opinion from cautious choice or their own myopic attitude.

A chief complaint made against these early post-prohibition wines was the vinegary taste. Such taste was indicative of numerous extremely poor cellar practices, if not outright fraudulent neglect.

In response to the public outcry the new Ontario board instituted a ruling which permitted only one part of volatile acid (vinegar) in 400 parts. Immediately half of those prohibition opportunist wineries

Chapter IV

closed their doors. They couldn't even meet such basic requirements.

One part in 400 of volatile acid, although producing somewhat of a cleansing affect on the industry, was still not much of a standard for acids. It still allowed for a tasteable trace of vinegar. However, to have set standards any higher might have been to close down all but a handful of wineries, certainly the vast majority of the industry.

But the industry was on the move; not all were going out of business. A great deal of market consolidation took place with many of the poachers falling by the wayside. In the meantime imported wines of quality were making points with Canadian consumers gaining a larger and larger share of the market.

Shortly after becoming the new head of Ontario's Liquor Control Board, Sir Henry Drayton instituted a school designed to teach Canadian winemakers how to make wine. For some it was to be a revelation, for others it was an elementary refresher course, nothing more. But it was to take its toll. For again the number of wineries was virtually cut in half as many just dropped out.

So, more than teach those who already knew how to make a fine wine product, the notorious Drayton school went a long way to refine the industry still further.

And by the early thirties, the Board began to tighten up even more. The old complaint of a hint of vinegar was eliminated completely as the Board set new standards of volatile acids which lowered their levels to that below human ability to sense its presence. Water restrictions were enforced to control the amounts added to the juice or must. Two hundred and fifty gallons of wine became the maximum quantity you could wring out of a ton of grapes. And hygiene regulations were upgraded and were to be strictly enforced.

And yet with all of the positive steps forward, within the industry, other obstacles were being created between the producer and the consumer. For it was becoming even more difficult to get their products to the consumer.

By now the country had begun to feel the pinches of the depression. And by the mid thirties it would be tightly embraced by it. Hardly a fortuitous time to sell what was still considered a luxury item for most Canadians. And then, one with such a questionable reputation.

Coupled with this was the fact that even though the temperance movement had lost the war they were still fighting a number of delaying actions. Negative attitudes towards wine in this land were going to die hard. By the mid 1970's traces of this temperance view could still be felt in subtle ways. Most evident in restrictive laws towards places of consumption.

Another major difficulty had become evident - the logistics of distribution. Of course, wine was available in the Liquor Board outlets. Yet, this poor cousin, wine, amidst all its stronger relatives, in the way of spirits, found it difficult to compete. The atmosphere in Board outlets was certainly not conducive to selling wine. And Liquor Boards were not known for their flair in using attractive merchandising displays. During this era the only shape you were likely to see on display in any Liquor Store, which even resembled a bottle, might be one of the staff - at least until you made your purchase.

The shift now in population from rural areas to the cities made it even more difficult to make full use of the retail store each winery was permitted to operate. With many of these notorious wineries 'going under', the Board encouraged the industry to consolidate even further. By overseeing the purchase of the smaller wineries, by producers who had the expertise and finances needed for a healthy industry, the Liquor Board prompted the Canadian wine industry to take another giant step forward.

Little in the way of tangible assets or goodwill accrued to the buyers except the obvious advantage of gaining another retail outlet for their products; yet by law these outlets were umbilically tied to the winery. However, **disconnective** legislation soon arrived. They could now move their retail outlets to the consumer. Yet in Ontario, L.C.B.O. caution still prevailed and the decision of maintaining only one store for every license given out was retained.

Some wineries, now well established, had purchased a dozen or more competitors and of course, were allotted as many retail outlets. In Ontario the number of retail wine stores operated apart from L.C.B.O. outlets stagnated at 51. If an ideal new retail location became available to a producer he must then close down another of his locations to make the new one available. A ludicrous situation but one visible remnant of lingering "temperance" influence.

"War is Hell", one man said. And it didn't do much to help the wine industry either. Even in Europe wine production during World War II 1939-1945 felt the ill affects of the pugnacious side of man's character.

On the western side of the Atlantic the industry didn't suffer from direct abuse to its acreage. But supply shortages halted much in the way of expansion and progress. It made it very difficult for some to survive financially during these years and equally as difficult for those who preferred European wines - they could rarely get a bottle.

Bottles, caps, sugar, wood or cardboard for packaging, even new cuttings were difficult commodities to lay your hands on. The war effort consumed such items with an insatiable appetite.

The more hardy and determined wineries weathered these shortages and the war years. Now, pushed by growing public demand for better wines, and an increased sophistication in wine taste the Canadian industry began to move positively forward. It was winning friends, again, often more for patriotic reasons than good taste, but they were still friends. The shortage of European wines didn't hurt either.

Whenever a disagreement exists between two parties one sure-fire method of setting it aside is to introduce a third party, as a common enemy. The rift that prohibition had established between the Canadian wine industry and the consumer was immeasurably assisted in its healing processes by the growing introduction of "imported" or "foreign" wines.

After the war, came an influx of European immigrants. Immigration officials saw to it that they didn't bring much of their local wine with them, but they couldn't stop them importing a taste for the wines of Europe.

Canadian wines were not attractive to them. The strange pungent taste and aroma bore little resemblance to the vinifera wines they had grown up with. And so demands for the importation of European wines increased. Significant quantities began to come ashore and found willing new converts in the manner of those Canadians who had so long rejected the local product. The softer, more subtle elegance of European Vinifera wines was more suited to their palates. Many Canadian soldiers that had fought in the European **theatre** also brought back with them a taste for the elegant, distinguished table wines of Europe.

But like that third party, for some, these imports bore a distinct threat to our native industry. Now, Canadian wines became something to protect, with the same vigor they would the sovereignty of Canadian soil.

So wine opinions started to polarize in our land. The Canadian industry seemed only too willing to grasp at this new consumer support. They sponsored and fostered the idea that although Canadian wines were different they also represented a high quality product, but simply of a unique variety - and that personal taste was the final arbiter of wine quality. The old "if you like it, it's a great wine" routine.

This attitude became so prevalent during the fifties and very early sixties it seemed Labrusca and Concord would become an integral and symbolic part of Canadiana . . . like Maple Syrup.

European importers and the consumers of Vinifera wines were not innocent bystanders to these events. Their constant barrage of destructive criticism directed at Canadian wines served to only further polarize the issue and the followers. Some criticism was legitimate but other complaints were merely absurd accusations from a certain segment of Canadian society who used wine as a social yardstick. To be caught in the company of anyone drinking a Canadian wine let alone be seen drinking any yourself was tantamount to striking your name from a number of social registers.

Yet the sails of both these untenable attitudes were soon to be deflated by one factor - economics.

There was no question, taste preference in Canada was steadily moving away from the stronger native Labrusca grape taste. As well, sweeter wines were falling on poor times. Lighter, drier table wines were gaining popularity at a phenomenal rate.

From the mid to late sixties imported wine sales consistently advanced by greater percentages than domestic brands. Sometimes by twice as much. They were gaining a larger and larger share of the market. In 1964 Canadian wines held 75% of the entire Canadian market. By 1975 it had dropped to 61% of the market.

The Canadian producers realized they would have to shift their emphasis from Labruscas to hybrids and locally-grown viniferas if they were to survive. The continued decline in dessert wine sales

Chapter IV

and growing table wine consumption was soon to be echoed by what the Canadian industry was to offer the consumer.

With growing world demand for the more famous European labels, prices for these wines shot up with little warning. The relatively fixed output of many of the famous European vineyards created a buying competition among some nations.

Some, frequently thought of as "emerging" nations, where wine is concerned, were just beginning to get acquainted with the grape. And in these lands too, wine was also becoming one of those social yardsticks. At the same time these attitudes were on the wane in our own land.

As a result, a subtle shift in marketing approaches began to manifest itself among the importing fraternity. Gradually, wine was becoming the drink for the average person, regardless of social or economic status.

Consequently, a larger and larger share of new wine listings allotted to importers were obtained for wines in the lower quality **reasonably** priced category. Even some listings for higher quality wines were sacrificed for lower ones. Most if not all, of the great individual brand success stories (introducing a label and having it skyrocket from a sales standpoint) still occur with lower priced wines. The average wage earner is now the target of virtually all 'imported' wine advertising. 'Elite' wines with their static production levels have little problem selling out each vintage. It's the more common everyday wines that need that extra boost from a public relations and advertising program.

The imperative questions today are still what do the respective wine factions have to offer the Canadian wine public? How do they measure up? What about new Canadian wines - are they any good? Can you trust all imports?

These and many more questions are commonly asked about wine; in fact 100 of the wine questions Canadians ask most often are answered directly in the next section of this book . . . based on the syndicated wine column "Wine View", by Andrew Sharp.

SECTION II

Questions and Answers

- From Grapes to Wine
- How to Treat Wine
- Wine Accessories
- A Wine Vocabulary
- Wine and Food - The Perfect Partners
- Wine and Health
- Canada
- France
- Italy
- Germany
- Other Vinelands
- Wines With a Kick

Chapter V

From Grapes to Wine

Q. How are grapes manufactured into wine and who invented it?

A. Grapes simply do what comes naturally . . . make wine. That may sound somewhat facetious, but contrary to some views, the natural offspring of grapes is wine not grape juice.

Grapes To Wine

Indeed, it's grape juice that has to be more 'manufactured' or chemically treated to prevent it from transforming itself into wine. The ever so 'natural' product of the vine is wine.

SUGAR + YEAST = ALCOHOL + CARBON DIOXIDE. That's the rudimentary way of expressing the chemical reaction which transforms grapes into wine. The sun forms sugar in the grape. Collected on each grapeskin are millions upon millions of airborne yeasts, moulds and bacteria. When fresh grapes are crushed the yeasts begin to feed upon the sugars in the grape juice, transforming it into alcohol, carbon dioxide and a few hundred other minor chemical substances. The carbon dioxide gas dissipates into the air and you are left with a mildly alcoholic beverage, WINE.

Rather raw, crude wine admittedly, but nonetheless, wine. Many refinements have been added over the centuries to control and improve this natural wonder. Yet scientists still do not completely understand all the chemical reactions that take place during fermentation. Oenologists (little old wine-makers) merely lend a guiding hand over this intriguing reaction. With tender care and skillful handling they ease it through various stages, bottle it, age it and then at just the right moment it becomes available to you, the ultimate consumer.

The oldest record of wine is the Biblical reference in Noah's time (circa 2400 B.C.). Since he already knew how to make wine we might assume the techniques had been passed on to him.

Rather than anyone 'inventing' wine a more accurate description or word might be 'discovered'. Since fermentation is a natural occurrence all someone had to do was to step or sit on a bunch of grapes and off they went - into the 'wonderful world of wine'.

Q. Does wine get better when it gets older?

A. Do you? I don't want to appear flippant, but that's a relevant question. Despite T.V. commercials that tell you, "You're not getting older, baby, just better," we eventually realize, that only happens in Hollywood.

Wine - Its Life Cycle

We are born, grow to physical maturity, reach our peak, perhaps travel on a plateau for a time and from there on, it's downhill into the rocking chair. Wine is no exception. In this respect, wine is very human. Wine has its youth, its adolescence, its maturity and at length it invariably declines into senility.

How long each of these stages may last, for any particular wine, rests upon many variables. Humans are quite similar. Some of us are ready for a **Home** by our forties. While others are just getting warmed up to life.

For wine, much stands or falls on the variety of grape. Certain grapes breed wines that are over the hill in a couple of years. Yet, others need fifty years before they hit their peak of maturity. The trick is to know when a wine has reached its peak and to drink it before it starts to decline. And just to keep you on your toes, each year or vintage, this pattern or life cycle may vary for each grape, due to climate, soil conditions and geography.

So it becomes vital to know which grape was used in producing the wine, how old it is, where it was grown and the prevailing weather conditions in the area that year. Then, if you really know your stuff, you just might be able to ascertain the best time to enjoy this vintage.

But don't be overly concerned. Ninety percent of all the wines in the world are ordinary wines that should be drunk before their third birthday, or sooner.

Beaujolais for example, is a wine born to be consumed in its youth, for then it is at its peak. With rare exception, to wait more than three years would be a waste. Bordeaux and Burgundies range anywhere from four to a dozen years before they reach their heights, sometimes more. And Ports, why, some take half a century before they burst forth in full bloom.

So age . . . it can be both friend and foe to wine, as it can be to us. But that's half the joy . . . the chase . . . the quest for that perfect moment to savour a wine that has achieved its fullest stature. Such efforts are never unrewarding.

Q. How important is yeast in wine-making?

A. Next to grapes it's number one on the "importance" scale.

Saccharomyces Ellipsoideus (Wine Yeasts)

Yeasts are airborne unicellular microorganisms that collect on the skin of the grape. When the grapes are crushed the yeasts react with the grape sugar to make alcohol and thusly wine. Some yeasts produce higher alcohol levels than others.

This is of course, a grossly over-simplified and a rather sterile description of the chemical processes that take place in fermentation.

Actually yeast plays an unheralded role in producing the end character and flavour of the wine. On the skin of any freshly picked grape you will find thousands of different types of yeasts and bacteria, some beneficial, others definitely harmful to wine production.

However, in any given vineyard region one strain of yeast may be dominant, demonstrating an ability to overpower all other yeasts during fermentation. This one dominant yeast, if beneficial, shares in producing the unique character that may distinguish wines from that region.

In modern wine production they take little chance with wild yeasts. Only a specific yeast is used. That particular regional yeast is isolated and cultured separately so that when added to the freshly squeezed juice you get a relatively pure reaction. And one that is consistently unique to that region.

Canadian wine producers primarily use yeasts indigenous to European vineyards - for their more desirable qualities. A great deal of research is being done on yeasts at Canada's Vineland Research Station to isolate a truly distinctive yeast, peculiar to our vineyards. Hope still prevails that such research will some day also produce a microorganism that will remove the "foxy" flavour and aroma from our native Canadian grapes. If that happens a cheer will go up from the Niagara grapegrowers loud enough to be heard in Newfoundland.

Q. Does the ageing of wine in wooden barrels actually improve it?

A. Much depends upon the wine - some wines die of advanced age not long after they leave the fermenting vats.

Wooden Casks

For the most part ageing wine in wooden casks or barrels is a specific step designed to improve the wine, while it just so happens to get a little older in the process. But you can overdo it!

On occasion if a wine stays in "cask" too many months it can become "withered" or "seche" as the French say. Or, perhaps it may even become "oaky" or "woody" - it simply takes on too much of the taste of the oak.

Wine ages more quickly in cask and for red wines of at least 'noble' quality 1 to 3 years is with rare exception, the maximum stay before

A Bordeaux cooper plying his ancient art.

bottling . . . where it may continue to age and improve more slowly for years or decades to come. White wines are usually out of wood and resting quietly in bottle anywhere from 3 to 18 months after they are vinted.

And much depends on the type of cask or barrel, too. Oak is by far superior. Chestnut and Redwood are acceptable in some circles, but are simply not in the same class when it comes to use with truly fine or great wines. Renowned wines the world over owe much of their reputation to the fact they were aged properly in quality oak casks.

Different producers and specific wine regions all have their favourite types of oak, as well . . . like the famous Limousin oak used exclusively in the Cognac region. An international favourite in North America and Europe is Tennessee White Oak.

Some producers of great Burgundies and Bordeaux use new casks for each vintage. The second-hand casks go for use with wines of less fame. But many producers will reuse the same casks for several vintages before they are replaced.

Q. Which are better - corks or plastic caps?

A. It all depends on what you're trying to cork - a chateau-bottled Bordeaux or a quart of local hooch.

Corks versus the Cap

The growing move away from corks made from the bark of the Quercus Suber (better known as the Cork Oak tree) to plastic caps has upset its fair share of wine traditionalists. Yet, for the most part, they have little to complain about.

At least 90% of the wine produced each year is common wine, to be consumed as soon as it is bottled. To put anything except a convenient, cheap cap on them would be a waste of time, money and trees.

But, for some wines a cork made from the Cork Oak is definitely more desirable. The 'cork theorem' goes something like this - "the longer the anticipated lifespan of the wine, the better and longer the cork you need."

Many wines are quite capable of ageing beneficially in bottle. For, these wines, corks are a must. A quality cork permits enough slow evaporation and minute oxidation to add measurably to the bouquet and distinction of the wine.

The average lifespan of a long, quality cork is about 20 years, after which it should be replaced. Wines like Beaujolais, meant to be drunk in their youth, you will note, have a much shorter cork than say, a vintage Burgundy.

When you open a bottle and notice that the top of the cork, just under the foil capsule, is moist and mouldy, don't be too alarmed. This is quite natural and happens often.

It doesn't mean the wine is bad. And sniffing wine corks is largely a pompous farce. Anything the cork can tell you about the wine, the wine can tell you better itself. What little can be learned from the cork is more meaningful to the professionals · consumers can essentially forget sniffing them.

That's unless, of course, you get your jollies out of sniffing corks.

Q. Is there any significance to the shape of wine bottles?

A. Shape can say a lot · for people and bottles. The shape of a wine bottle can even occasionally hint at the contents.

Bottles and More Bottles

While the traditional European wine countries held a virtual monopoly on world wine trade · the shape of the bottle had something to say. Today, with more than thirty lands involved in a commercial wine production, the picture becomes somewhat blurry.

Yet, some broad generalities can be made. Two of the most renowned bottle shapes in all of the wonderful world of wines come from France.

The traditional high-shouldered, short-necked bottle is the style made famous and used in the Bordeaux region of France exclusively (fig. 3). This representative of Bordeaux has spread to many other areas in the world. Many of the better Italian wines use a similar design. Most lands that market a Bordeaux or Claret TYPE of wine use this traditional shape. But be assured with the exception of some California varietals, the only similarity they share with a genuine Bordeaux wine is the shape of the bottle.

Probably the world's champion bottle shape is the classic slope-shouldered Burgundy bottle (fig. 2.). Burgundy wines have come packaged in this style bottle for generations. Even in France, other wine districts like Languedoc, the Rhone district, the Loire and so on, have poached this design. Like a juicy rumour, the classic Burgundy bottle has spread to every wine producing nation in the world. The similarities end there, though.

There are several other great shapes, in bottles that is, that we could discuss. Five distinct shapes seem to be emerging as the world standards. We've considered two very briefly and will not omit the other three, but their pictures will have to suffice on this occasion. (Fig. 1-5 on page 64)

Q.   Can other fruits make a true wine?

A.   Can you get orange juice out of tomatoes?

Wine or Not Wine?

With a little sugar, some yeast, and a few splashes of water you can ferment almost anything, including last night's leftovers. And over the centuries someone, somewhere has tried to make wine out of almost everything known to man.

Some professionals and many basement buffs regularly ferment a beverage out of carrots, dandelions, cherries, blueberries, honey and various other fruits and vegetables. But should these beverages be labelled wine?

Opinions are diverse over this question, with little unity of thought evident over the years. So, mine is a singularly personal view. And it's no!

Fermented grape juice, in my opinion, holds the sole right to be labelled wine - for several good reasons. Firstly it has an historical claim to the term. Grapes as no other fruit, have been made into

Chapter V

wine for some 4,000 years.

All of the ingredients needed to transform grapes into wine are naturally present in the grape itself. Other fruits need liquid, yeast or sugar in differing amounts to make it economical. And volume! If you took all the liquid of all other substances which are claimed to be turned into wine you wouldn't have enough moisture to dampen all the labels used on wine bottles.

Don't get me wrong though - many other substances can produce very palatable, enjoyable beverages. But they're not wine!

Q. Can you make really fine wines at home?

A. Unless your home is in the middle of a vineyard, probably not.

Home-Made Wines

You must realize it's not without some personal risk I even discuss this question - as I have several close friends who are avid 'basement wine-makers.'

This is an extremely sensitive area to explore because so many home wine-makers put so much of themselves, their time, tender care and feelings into each batch, to direct one adverse comment at the fruitage of their labours becomes tantamount to assailing motherhood.

Yet with these risks involved we'll plunge ahead. Despite irresponsible claims of potential greatness by those who market the products used in home production, the realistic plateau for the vast majority of amateur wine-makers is that of vin ordinaires, at best. This is not a slam against such persons. Considering what raw materials are available to them, it's a compliment.

And that's the key - or lack of it we might say. Fresh grapes that father fine or even average wines are not readily available throughout the world. They command high prices. Little if any are ever available to the public. Grapes that are exported from California are usually those, commercial wineries wouldn't use for wine production. They're table grapes, really.

Even concentrates benefit the home buff little. Firstly, high quality grapes are rarely if ever made into concentrates. So the enthusiast is faced with a concentrate from grapes that are poor at best. And secondly, once any grape is made into a concentrate, wines of mediocrity are their ultimate aspiration. So it's material availability not lack of skill and desire that holds back the amateur.

Yet, if everyday drinking wines, at prices Liquor Boards can only dream of, is what you want - **vivre les basement vignerons!**

Q. How do they arrive at the different names for wines?

A. One might be tempted to guess that a room full of ad agency type genuises sat around dreaming them up, but this is rarely the case.

Brand, Generic and Varietal

Three sources provide the vast majority of names found on wine labels. The rest . . . well, we can probably ignore them and feel assured we've missed little if anything in life.

Brand names (sometimes called house labels or monopoles) are experiencing a world-wide resurgence due to the international economic climate. With wine prices spiralling ever upward the call for respectable table wines, of dependable quality, at reasonable prices has mushroomed. To fill this growing need, wine merchants are marketing more wines wearing house labels. The name will have no legally defined meaning. The reputation of the shipper and the name itself becomes known to the public and a clientele is built up for this brand. Because of massive, even inter-regional blending these wines will forever be vin ordinaires. Yet, they should be consistent in quality from year to year and do fill a real gap.

Reputable shippers take great care to protect the quality of such wines in order to protect sales. Some good examples are the world popular red wine, Prefontaine and the German white, Black Tower - both dependable everyday wines at yesterday's prices.

Generic names are those like Sherry, Burgundy, Bordeaux, Champagne, Port, Chianti, Chablis, etc. They are most frequently associated with distinct areas of production and by rights should be

Chapter V

kept exclusive to that region. However, many other countries outrightly poach these names but rarely, if ever, do the imitators meet the original mark. Like most imitations, they would be better avoided, unless you're willing to accept them for what they aren't.

More and more Varietal wines abound today. These are wines named after the grape used to vint them. They are generally honest in what they present. But some caution is advisable. The same grape will be very different from land to land and because of blending, they can be very ordinary wines. Some names to look for are Riesling, Gamay, Pinot Noir, Chardonnay, Cabernet Sauvignon, etc.

Further caution should be exercised in ascertaining if the varietal wine you buy is 100% the variety named on the label. More and more countries are legally allowing producers to keep varietal labels on wines that are blended with other grape varieties - some could only have 51% of the named grape. Though legal and growing, it's a detestable practice - a stain on the whole wine industry.

Q. Does the year printed on a wine label really make a difference?

A. It has about the same importance as the one on your birth certificate. It may or may not say a lot.

Vintage

I'm sure you'll agree there are many aspects, good and bad to the subject of age. Wine is no exception and it would be the height of presumption on my part to even attempt to list all such aspects of age and wine in one article, let alone discuss them. So we'll look at one aspect only - why some wines have vintage dates and others don't.

Two distinct philosophies dominate the wine industry - vintages and blending. Some producers choose to bottle the wine of each year separately, labelling and marketing it as that year, that vintage. These producers are subject to the whim of each season. Good, poor or bad they essentially have to live with it. Their advantage - when it is a good year they send a vastly superior wine to market.

If consumers are on their toes they can pick and choose years that are better than others.

Other producers are not so venturesome of spirit and choose to even out the variables a little. By blending the vintages of different years they can bottle and market a product of fairly consistent quality, year after year. But buy eliminating chances of those poor or bad years, blending also curtails all potential superior or great years. It evens matters out to a respectable level of mediocrity.

The consumer can balance the merits of each philosophy and choose a wine to serve his or her particular purpose and budget.

Q. Is the Clarity of a wine a judge of its quality?

A. Bottled water is usually crystal clear · but that doesn't say much for its quality or taste. So it is with wine.

Clarity

North Americans, with their occasionally weird palates, have been chiefly responsible for wineries having to upgrade their clarification processes . . . to a degree that can go a little beyond reason. If a wine isn't 'crystal' clear, they assume something is wrong. They erroneously conclude · the clearer the better.

Before we take any further steps in this topic I should make it clear, that I am not advocating that cloudy wines are acceptable. A relative clarity is more usually synonymous with a fine wine · as steps taken to achieve 'crystal' clarity can lower the true quality and stature of a wine.

Clarifying wine is nothing new. The Romans and other ancient wine-making nations added a variety of substances (fining agents) to the wine to clear it. Blood, egg whites and milk were popular. These would settle to the bottom taking most of the suspended particles with them.

They worked quite well and left the wine acceptably clear. Some smaller particles were left, naturally, but nothing you'd have to use a toothpick on.

More modern fining agents now predominantly used by wineries

Chapter V

are isinglass, geletine, a number of clays such as Bentonite, spark-alloids and even beechwood chips.

To some this wasn't enough and various forms of filtration were devised. Some beneficial to the wines, others not. The wines are passed through a variety of different types of filters, eliminating particles up to any given size. Asbestos filters are growing in popularity despite inherent dangers from the asbestos itself. The asbestos filter is normally covered in a silk bag to filter out any asbestos fibres.

Too severe a filtration can "numb" a wine, take the life out of it, subtracting many of its better qualities. Yet to many white wines it is a blessing - but overall moderation is the better course. So a 'brilliantly' clear wine will not necessarily indicate a quality wine.

Q. How do they make wines bubbly?

A. It all depends on whether you want round, oblong or square bubbles.

Bubbles

For some strange reason bubbles bring so many things to life. Just think of how many of our traditional favourites would never have made it without bubbles. Flat beer - never. Still soda pop - unthinkable. And what would a bubble bath be without bubbles?

Bubbles in wine can be the result of three different processes. One is good, one is all right and the other - well, it's bubbly to say the best for it.

The 'good' one is the result of a natural second fermentation that takes place in the bottle. True Champagne is made in this manner. In fact, the process is labelled "Methode Champenoise". The bubbles are small and give almost a creamy 'mousse' texture to the wine. Round bubbles we might say, symbolically-speaking.

The "Charmat method" of making wine bubbly is a takeoff of the bottle fermentation only on a much larger scale. A second, natural fermentation is achieved in large tanks and then the wine is bottled. Not bad, the bubbles are somewhat larger and coarser,

Dégorgement - removing the sediment. By freezing the neck, sediment is frozen in a slug of ice, then popped out.

oblong might describe their texture.

The 'poor' bubbly comes from the injection of carbon dioxide gas into the wine. Not only is this the cheap way out but it's fast too, great for the production line. Only wines of the cheaper or "pop wine" classification use such a method. The wine is usually as cheap as the method. The bubbles are large, coarse, almost square, so to speak. They taste like you'd imagine a chicken feels when laying a square egg.

Q. Which are better wines, dry or sweet?

A. Your personal taste is the final judge, but I wouldn't suggest a dry Bordeaux with your next dessert nor a Sauterne with your next steak. The conflict might lead to an internal rebellion.

Dry or Sweet

Getting the ideal, balanced viewpoint on any subject seems to be an impossible task - wine is no exception.

For years Canadians who have a penchant for sweets in general were used to drinking wines on the sweeter side, Sherries, Ports and so on. Then along came the hue and cry for European wines and the increased popularity of dry table wines was upon us. Almost with a vengeance some Canadian wine drinkers have turned against all sweet wines as if they were the sole cause of tooth decay.

In truth, there is balance needed in one's viewpoint towards dry and sweet wines. Ever since North Americans started inviting wine to the dinner table, drier table wines have taken an increased share of overall wine sales. And to date they deservedly have the lion's portion, and are still growing.

Outlets that list wines according to relative sweetness often aid in giving the impression that wine should be judged and purchased by such sweet or dry standards alone. When really, both dry and sweet wines have their appropriate place in any well rounded wine repertoire. Indeed many of the most famous wines in the world are sweet wines: Sherry, Port, Sauterne, Madeira, Marsala, etc.

Wines which are characteristically drier usually go best with the main course, while wines sweeter in nature are better served at the end of the meal.

So, "better" only applies to dry and sweet wines when you consider what company they're keeping - unless you personally have a weird sense of taste you have to pacify.

Q.   How important is the colour of a wine?

A.   Unlike people, the colour of wine can be very revealing.

Colour

To begin with, the infinite variations in shadings of wine colours are more important to the expert, the wine professional. It's part of his job to know what they mean. To the novice or even the wine-lover who appreciates fine wines, colour differences render more general judgment. Some of the basics are worth noting, though.

To get a proper view of the colour, tilt the glass against a background of a white tablecloth, a candle or some other relatively uncoloured light source . . . daylight from the North is actually best according to expert wine judges. Or you can use the silver 'tastevin' (that shallow silver cup) in the Burgundian fashion.

Some Basics:

Whites from cooler districts, Germany, Austria, Northern Italy - the colour of pale straw and that of gold with a greenish tinge perhaps. Whites from Bordeaux, Southern Italy - could be as golden coloured as ripe corn, little or no touch of green.

In most white table wines any hint of amber or brown indicates age or with younger wines that they have been exposed to too much oxygen. Sweet white wines should be gold in hue, not brown, unless very old.

Red wine colouring ranges from purple (most often a young and very poor wine) through Burgundy Reds, brick reds to crimson-brown like that of fall leaves. This range of shadings is too infinite to describe

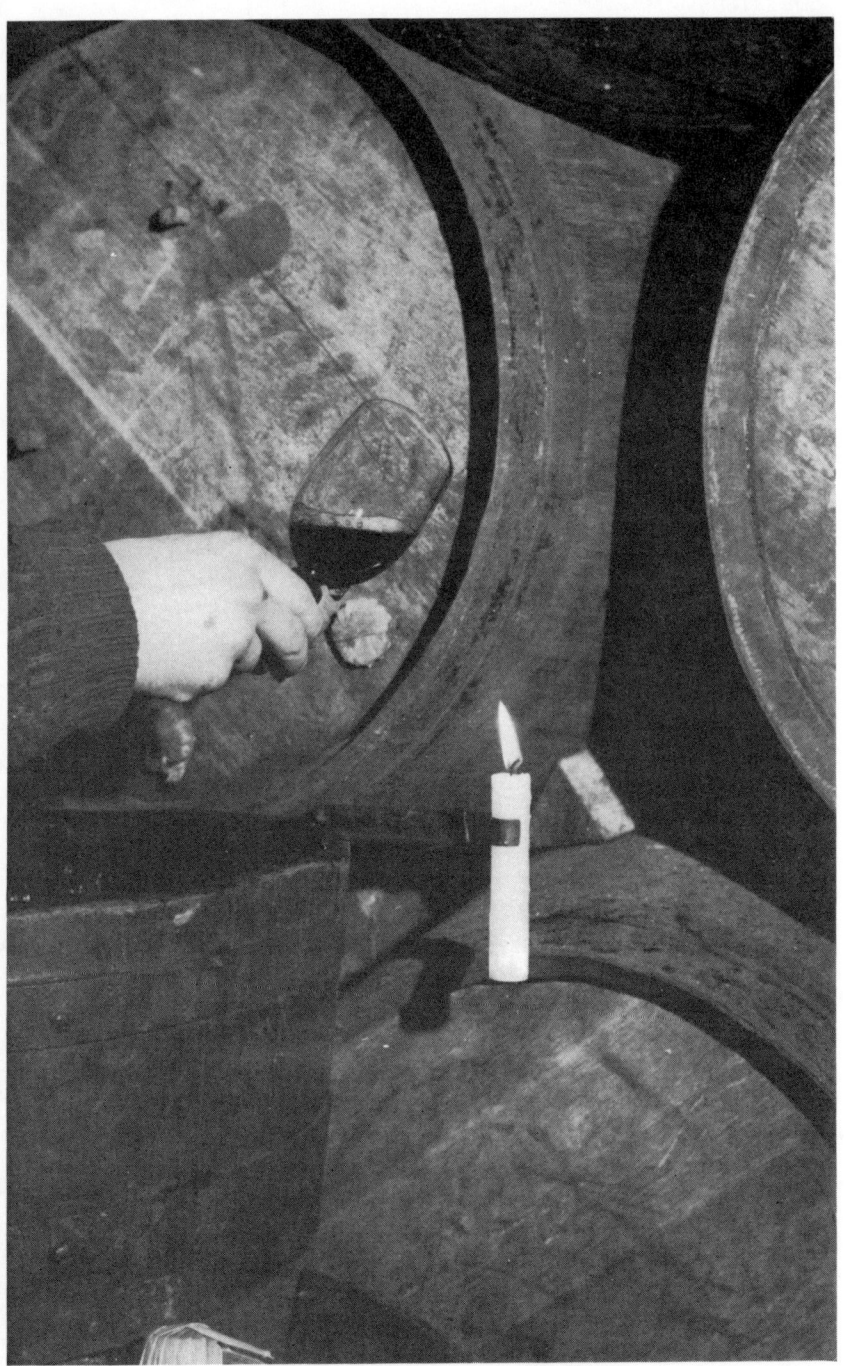

Candling the wine for colour and clarity.

here. The brownish tinge can be noted just at the edge of the wine in a tilted glass and is often indicative of fine wines of advanced age. Nothing to be alarmed about unless you know the wine is a young wine. Then, our friend oxidation has again been at work.

Rosés have their differences too - from strawberry pink to almost orange. Neither end of the spectrum is desirable. Too pink and it's poor wine to start with. Too orange and senility is upon it.

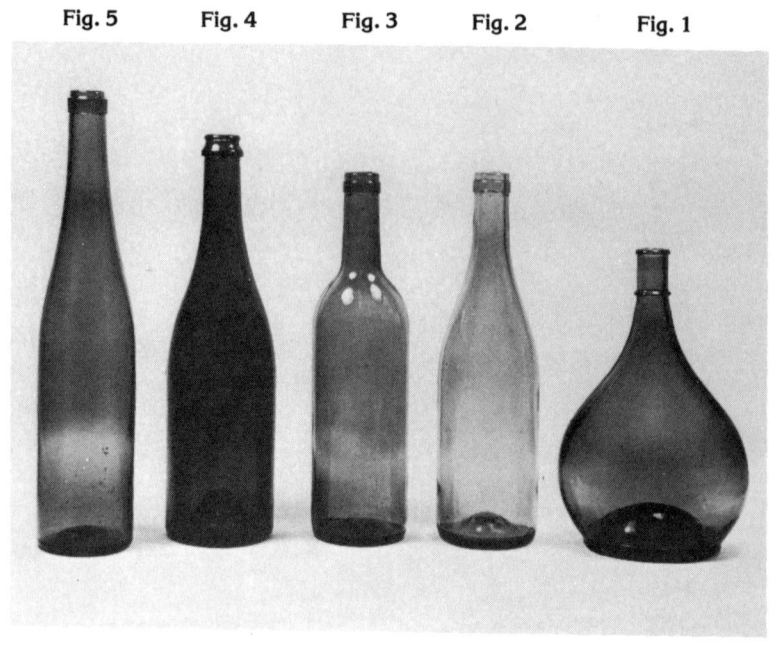

Fig. 5	Fig. 4	Fig. 3	Fig. 2	Fig. 1
German White Italian White	Champagne Sparkling wines (heavier glass)	Bordeaux Claret Classico Chianti	Burgundy Loire Rhone Provence	Flagon-type Rosés

Chapter VI

How To Treat Wine

Q. What is the best place to store wine?

A. If other members of the family enjoy wine, where they can't find it. However, if they are trustworthy and not known wine-nappers, a cool, dark corner is best.

Wine Storage

When speaking of the ideal place to store your wines, we again run into what may be considered ideal, compared with what may be practical for you. Whether ideal and practical turn out to be one in the same depends on how much you are willing to invest in a wine storage area.

Ideally, you should have an area that is temperature controlled. If a small room is available, some people use thermostatically controlled refrigeration units to maintain the desired temperature. Others buy special cabinets that are already equipped this way and especially designed for wine storage. These cost the price of many, many bottles of wine, I might add. Unless you have a collection of fine wines that you want to keep for a number of years, all this is quite a luxury.

If you simply like to keep a few bottles of everyday wine around, with perhaps the odd bottle of something special for certain occasions, you can get away with much less. But there are definitely some no-no's to avoid.

Light, over a period of time, can adversely affect wine . . . so, darkness is preferable. When considering temperatures and wine storage, remember it's not so much the wrong temperature that deteriorates your wine, but fluctuations in temperature. Generally, the best temperature range is 50 to 60 degrees F. But 45 to 75 degrees F. is acceptable if it remains constant. Vibrations can also affect your wine, so avoid any such area.

So, some definite no-no's would be the basement floor next to the clothes dryer, in or on top of the refrigerator and near any doors that open to the outside frequently. Many fruit cellars are perfect but if you live in an apartment the back of a closet might also do.

Whatever, choose the spot that is closest to the ideal requirements and you'll avoid some nasty surprises when you do open that special bottle.

Q. Which is the proper way to serve wine?

A. Without spilling it all over your guest! At least, that should be your foremost goal.

Serving Wine

Some seem to thrive on pomp and ceremony more than others. If you want to accompany that special bottle of wine with a peeling blast of trumpets, that's up to you and the trumpeters. But others are content serving wine in teacups. And that's okay too, if the teacups don't leak.

As with all manners, their soul lies in common sense and a sincere desire to make those around you feel at ease. Removing the cork and serving your guest or companion without mishap is the major task at hand. Accomplishing this in a comfortable, relaxed manner is all that is needed. No ceremony is more appropriate.

Too much pomp and ceremony will not add to the ultimate goal, of enjoying the wine for its own sake. Rather, it will frequently add to the stress of the situation. While everyone is breathlessly awaiting and watching your little serving ceremony, you can bet, that's when you'll blow it.

In restaurants that serve wine, most waiters appear to go through a confusing ritual when serving each bottle. Yet, it does have a practical purpose on most occasions. On the other hand it can be termed **buck-passing.**

When you've made your selection, the waiter will first return and present you with the bottle, label up. He does so to insure he has your correct choice, before he opens it. For, once he's pulled the cork, it's too late to change your mind, it's now your bottle. Then, of course, he pours an ounce or so for you to taste. Once you've agreed and nodded your approval - it really is your bottle, with no refunds on the empty. Now the **buck** is yours. Whether your choice of wine proved to be the right one or not, the price of that bottle will rightly appear on your check.

Of course, by approving the choice and tasting the wine first, you generally assure nothing is wrong with the wine and that you are getting what you paid for. This is the real purpose and a valid one at that.

Q.   At what temperature should you serve wine?

A.   Anything but at "room temperature."

Serving Temperatures

On too many bottles of red wine you'll find somewhere the serving suggestion "serve at room temperature". Ignore it! For the sake of the wine and your sense of taste.

For room temperature in a North American home (70-74 deg. F) is often considerably higher than room temperatures, say in France, Italy or even England, for that matter . . . the usual sources of this bright suggestion. Not to mention of course, in North America the room temperature in January and July may vary significantly. So in practical terms it's an impractical idea. But, is temperature all that important?

Yes! By all means. A red table wine overly chilled will be numbed, have little bouquet and will be quite astringent to the palate. On the other hand, a white table wine that is too warm can be virtually lifeless, dull and insipid. A few degrees can make a world of difference.

Reasonable parameters might be from 'iced' 38 deg. F. (in ice water) to 68 deg. F. Some very general serving temperatures:

Fine and great, red table wines	- 60-68 deg. F.
Lighter, more ordinary reds	- 58-62 deg. F.
Dry white and rosés	- 50-55 deg. F.
Sweeter whites and dessert wines	- 48-53 deg. F.
Sweet Sherries and Ports	- 60-65 deg. F.
Sparkling wines	- 38-45 deg. F.

To chill your wines you may choose an ice bucket or your refrigerator but the bucket is actually best. Refrigerator temperatures will vary somewhat from refrigerator to refrigerator. This usually depends upon how many children you have. The temperature of ice water is fairly consistent. And it keeps the bottled chilled while you're consuming the contents - good to the last cool drop.

Q. How do you arrange to have a wine tasting?

A. Somehow the slightest suggestion or hint that you're planning a wine tasting brings out more tasters than there are wines.

Tasting

There are three basic formats for wine tastings - professional, commercial and private. One is work, one is business, the other fun. If you're smart you'll avoid participating in the first, be wary of the second and never miss the third.

A professional tasting is work. It has a serious purpose behind it. The wine is literally tasted, not swallowed. For some it's their nine to five job, their profession. Interesting work perhaps, but it's hardly fun.

A commercial tasting is usually arranged by a producer or an importer. Here the merchant gathers together potential consumers,

The Good Wine Tasters. Hand-coloured lithograph by Claude Thielley (French, 1811-1891).

A Wine Shop. Etching and drypoint, Bror Julius Olsson Norfeldt (Swedish-American, 1855-1955).

usually large customers and frequently along, just for something to do, are members of the infamous media who write or talk about such topics.

The goal is to introduce, advertise and sell particular brands of wine. You are plied with both product and cordial, charming chit chat. These tastings are often enjoyable as they offer one the opportunity to taste a variety of different wines. But if you want to keep your balance, keep reminding yourself of the **raison d'etre** for this affair.

By far the more enjoyable of these three tastings, though rarely the most informative, are those private intimate little tastings. Certainly less formal and more relaxing they're an ideal excuse to get together with friends and four or five varieties of wine. The wine, some glasses, something to clean the palate (like crusty bread) and a few convivial hours to share are all that are really needed. And then taste on.

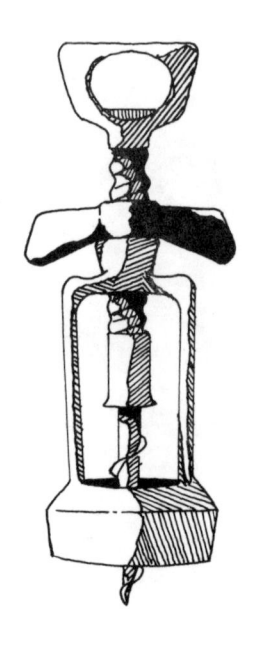

Chapter VII

Wine Accessories

Q. Are wine cradles of any advantage?

A. Having spent some time in a cradle myself, it's hard for me to remain totally objective. But, no, they have little real value - unless they are expensive.

Wine Accessories

There is nothing wrong with using a wine cradle, anymore than there would be with using your barbecue tongs to serve sugar cubes. If that's what you want, so be it.

It just so happens they are not really all that necessary or practical. With certain very old wines which may have a heavy sediment, a cradle can be of some value. Even then, it's best to decant such rare wines before serving.

Besides, cradles can be awkward. Just getting the bottle into some of these contraptions is no mean feat in itself. Like some children, they just don't want to go. So, spend the money it costs for a cradle on a bottle of wine, you'll be much happier.

A frequent companion to many a bottle of wine is a snow-white cloth wrapped around the neck and upper part of the bottle. Unless you enjoy washing red stains out of white linen or you're running a test on your laundry detergent, this is another little piece of pomp that lacks an honest purpose.

I use the word 'honest' because such cloths do have a practical purpose, if you're trying to hide the label. They accomplish that job rather well. Their appearance immediately makes me suspect of the wine and perhaps the host. What's he hiding?

As for their role of catching little dribbles that run down the side of the bottle: if you pour properly in the first place, you won't have dribbles. It's something like wearing a bib. As accident prone at the dinner table as I may be, I refuse to wear a bib on principle. It's been several years since I've used one and I simply don't intend to revert to the practice.

Q. What kind of glasses are the best to serve wine in?

A. The best glasses are those that don't leak. Beyond this simple, basic requirement, everything else is a bonus.

Wine Glasses

A glass does for wine what a gold setting does for a diamond or a gilt frame for a renowned painting.

Strictly speaking, glasses are unnecessary other than as a container. But what an elegant showcase they can provide for the indescribable spectrum of colours associated with wine.

Glasses with cut designs and those made from coloured or smoked glasses may be artful and in themselves something of beauty. However, if you desire to indulge the sense of sight to the full, by appreciating the infinite variances and shadings of wine colours, nothing should interfere. In fact, sight is one of the five senses used in determining the ultimate quality of any wine. So a glass that is crystal clear is the first requisite.

Now, look to the bowl of the glass. A TULIP shape is most desirable . . . where the lip is slightly less in diameter than the widest part of the bowl. Not only does this make it more difficult to spill the contents, in case you have a few clumsy guests around, but rather its main purpose is to concentrate or funnel the bouquet and aroma of the wine, to be more easily detected by the nose.

Chapter VII

Glasses that are stemmed provide another bonus. They give an elegant appearance, of course, but do have a more practical purpose. If held by the stem the wine in the glass doesn't get warmed by the heat of your hand. If you are drinking chilled wines, you'll especially appreciate this. Or if you're one of those persons who'd rather not leave fingerprints lying around, the stem is definitely the best place to grasp the glass.

The ideal glass then . . . crystal clear, tulip-shaped and stemmed. Oh, and it shouldn't leak!

Q. I can never seem to get a corkscrew that works properly. Any suggestions?

A. Finding a good corkscrew is like trying to find a good wife. When you do, hang on to them. They're hard to replace, and are becoming even more so as time goes along.

Corkscrews

Now, you might not think the subject of corkscrews and their various merits should occupy a significant place of interest in your life. But if you've ever pulled out the centre of a cork and had to dig out the rest with a kitchen knife, only to spray red wine on a white shirt or your best Irish linen table cloth, you may have more than a passing interest in them.

These unruly little monsters have probably produced more grief, ounce for ounce, than any gadget ever invented. Several things separate the good, the bad and the ugly -- corkscrew-wise.

The business end of the corkscrew is the "worm" itself. Find a good worm and half the battle is won. The worm or spiral should appear as if it had been wound around a centre shaft: the shaft being removed, creating a slot down the centre. But make sure the spiral is long enough . . . 2-1/2 to 3 inches.

The first time you pull up only the top half of the cork and end up pushing the rest down into the bottle, squirting wine over . . . you guessed it, you'll see the reason for a lengthy spiral.

Winning the other half of the battle depends on securing a

73

corkscrew with an effective method of leverage. The jackknife type used in restaurants (fig. 1) and the wing-style types, with two arms that are depressed, (fig. 2) work well and are the more dependable duo.

So, remember, if you find a good one, hang on to it. Never lend it out. Insist on opening every bottle yourself; and, of course, you might as well sample the contents while you're at it.

Q. Are those gadgets that pump air into the bottle reliable for removing corks?

A. Reliable? For blowing up balloons, maybe . . . but corks can be quite a different matter.

Cork-Removers

There seems to be two different styles of this type of cork-remover on the market. Both work on the same principle and both have a long hollow needle which is inserted down through the cork. One type utilizes a carbon-dioxide gas cartridge while the other depends upon you pumping the air in manually. Both share the appearance of a needle some sadistic horse doctor might employ.

The theory, albeit a sound one, is to pump air into the space between the bottom of the cork and the wine. The resulting pressure should gently force the cork upwards and out. So the theory goes . . . but you know how reliable some theories are.

Problems arise because no two corks are removed by the same pressure. Some corks are incredibly stubborn and refuse to yield to the maximum pressure these devices can develop. Some bottles have even exploded under such pressure.

But that's not the real problem, simply being defeated by a cantankerous cork. The real trick comes when, after your unsuccessful attempt, you remove the needle. With all that pressure still in the bottle often the wine comes shooting up the hole left by the needle, and you end up with a lovely spray of red wine . . . just like hitting an artesian well. And you can bet the wine will go somewhere you don't want it to.

Chapter VII

Then there are those corks that are comparatively loose. A little pressure from one of these devices and you've just launched your own cork into orbit. That's if you're fortunate enough to be outside at the time. If not, you'll usually find a little chip out of your plaster ceiling with a funny little red stain around it. Oh, well, it's always fun dreaming up stories to explain how it got there to the neighbours.

Although they do remove **some** corks, reliability is the key, so stick to the old dependables and you'll avoid disasters and ending up with three of them in the bottom of a drawer, like I have.

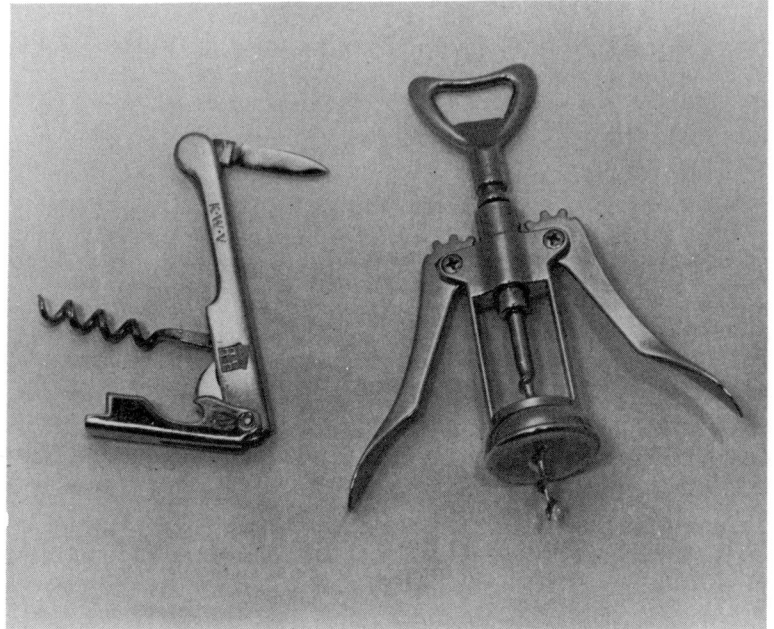

Fig. 1   **Fig. 2**

Jack-knife type   **Wing-style**
(waiters)   **(arms depressed)**

Chapter VIII

A Wine Vocabulary

Q What does it mean when you say a wine is dry? Does it mean it's sour?

A. When your glass is dry - it's empty. And when a well is dry - it's empty, too. But, when a wine is dry, that's something totally different. It could even be full.

Dry or Arid

Most of us automatically assume the opposite of sweet is sour. But in reality this is not the case. The opposite of sweet is a lack of sweetness. This might not appear as an overly profound statement, yet it bears consideration. For a lack of sweetness doesn't make something sour.

If you leave out the sugar in your favourite brownie recipe you may not appreciate the results but you couldn't describe them as being sour. Rotten, unfit for human consumption, maybe, but not sour. So when you speak of a dry wine, it's a wine without sweetness - an absence of sugar, not water.

If the wine fermentation process is allowed to follow, unhindered, its natural course, all the grape sugars are consumed by the yeasts and converted into alcohol. This invariably produces a dry wine - not sour, but dry. And indeed dry wines are the most natural.

So sweet and sour are adjectives well applied to some Chinese sauces and some individuals' personalities; but sour when descrip-

Chapter VIII

tive of wine usually means the wine has passed the point of no return. It's spoiled! Great for a salad but don't serve it to any of your friends in a glass, unless of course you intend to dry up a relationship.

Q. When someone talks about the "bouquet" of a wine - what are they talking about?

A. Certainly not an artistic grouping of grape-vine leaves in an elegant vase! In the common vernacular - the "smell" with a few twists thrown in just to keep you on your toes.

Bouquet and Aroma

The terms Bouquet and Aroma when used to describe wine do not mean one in the same thing. More than the fact that Bouquet is a longer and more elegant sounding word, the differences between it and **aroma** are considerably more profound.

Aroma describes the smell of the fruit; that particular grape used to vint that particular wine. So, when someone describes a wine as possessing a **fruity** smell, they are referring to its **aroma** and in a much lesser sense to its **bouquet.**

Young wines retain more of the smell of the original fruit than do older, well-aged wines. Thusly, they are more frequently described as being fruity or having a prominent aroma - like the famed Beaujolais.

Following fermentation, wine begins to age. The aroma begins to decline in prominence being subtly replaced by a growing, more complex smell - the bouquet. The bouquet of a wine is an orchestra of smells, a melange of fragrances derived from the alcohols, the fruits, the sugars and the many other constituents of fermented wine, that combine together to form its unique **bouquet.**

Aroma eventually becomes only one of many constituents formulating the bouquet. When a fine wine reaches full maturity the aroma becomes almost imperceptible. But the bouquet has reached full bloom and when uncorked will literally explode in your nostrils (no damage of course).

Q. When someone says of a wine "it is flowery" precisely what are they referring to?

A. A bouquet of wine fragrances!

"Flowers of the Vineyard"

"Flowery" is a very legitimate term in any wine vocabulary. With rarest exception, it's a description of singularly high praise meant to describe a certain aspect of a wine's overall bouquet.

Quite expectedly, it communicates to our noses a scent associated with that of fresh flowers. You will discover this "flowery" fragrance almost solely with white wines.

The classic example is that of the finer Moselle wines of Germany. Or, on rare occasions, other wines, also from the Riesling grape, grown in cool climates and on stoney soil, produce this special character and fragrance.

While we're at the "F's" in our wine dictionary it is also appropriate to clarify a term that is often misused and misunderstood - FULL. Frequently it is equated with the wine terms "heaviness" or "body". Wrong!

An illustration is the best way to define the term "full", with reference to wines. Compare heavy cream to skim milk, weightwise. Your first thought might be that the cream is heavier. Wrong again! Although the cream is thicker, ounce for ounce, the skim milk is heavier.

Now compare a light Alsatian white to a full red Burgundy. Which is heavier? The Alsatian? Right! As with oil and water - oil has a fuller texture but everyone knows which is lighter.

So "full" as a wine term is not synonymous with body or heaviness but refers only to texture. Though your wine may not be full, your glass should be.

Q. Balance and Body are terms I occasionally hear in reference to wine. Can you define them for me?

A. I'm glad you added "in reference to wine" otherwise I'd be competing with Mr. Webster and the Funk & Wagnalls team.

Balance and Body

Of course, what we're not talking about when we use the expression "body" is strange little particles floating around in your glass . . . at least not the kind you're likely to need a toothpick for.

This frequently misused wine term does not **only** refer to a wine that is high in alcohol, simply because that is descriptive of being **full-bodied**. Rather, full-bodied also denotes a wine that appears to our senses as having weight to it, not a light wine . . . not thin and watery but the opposite . . . having **substance** to it.

Determining if **full-bodied** is in itself beneficial or if it suggests a negative quality, depends very much upon what characteristics that particular wine should possess in the first place. A Champagne, a Riesling, Chablis or even a Beaujolais that is full-bodied would be considered a poor example of its type, by experts. While Barolo, big Burgundies and Chateauneuf-du-pape owe much of their fame to being full-bodied. They're the Charles Atlas' of the wine world.

Balance in wine is perhaps one of the more difficult wine expressions to define succinctly. For it has an illusive, chameleon-type meaning. Essentially, a wine that is balanced . . . is balanced, if you know what I mean. Oh, you don't? That's why you're reading this. Right! Anyway, it's a wine that possesses the particular characteristics it should possess, in the right proportions for that type of wine. So, a balanced wine could be quite ordinary but well **balanced** . . . if it had no obvious faults in its bouquet, flavour or aftertaste and so on.

And on the other hand a truly fine wine may have one of its qualities fall short of reasonable expectations but still be a superior wine when compared to a balanced ordinary wine. Understand? Anyway, I tried.

Q. When someone refers to 'acid' in a wine, just what are they talking about?

A. Don't get too worried - it's not something an impatient relative might slip into your drink to hasten the reading of the will.

Acid

And **acid** in wine has nothing to do with the use of this word to define the mind-bendng drug, LSD. The worst thing wine acid can do, if too plentiful, is bend your tastebuds a little out of shape.

Acid is a natural ingredient, to some degree, in all wines. But it needs balance. Too much and the wine is overly **tart.** Not enough and the wine would be described as "flat" or "dull." The proper balance gives wine life . . . without bending your tastebuds.

Four desirable types of natural acids can be found in wine, which in proper proportion contribute pleasing qualities to the wine - tartaric, citric, lactic and mallic acids. But that doesn't mean all acids are friendly. One acid in wine circles is considered wine enemy number one - **acetic acid** (when it passes certain levels).

The detectable presence of **acetic acid** is usually indicative of something amiss in the wine. Because the more common name for acetic acid is **vinegar**. And vinegar is the English word for the French expression **Vin aigre** meaning sour wine. Get the picture? If you don't your tastebuds will.

Even though acetic acid is present in most wines it is undetectable in amounts less than point one percent. Above this level and you can add a bottle of wine vinegar to your cupboard. Admittedly this may be an expensive way to buy wine vinegar but at least it'll be superior to any you buy at the supermarket .

Chapter IX

Wine & Food - the Perfect Partners

Q. Are there any rules that say which wines should go with certain foods?

A. None! But there are a few suggestions one is wise to consider.

Wine to Food

No one can dictate to you which wine you must serve with any particular dish. But if you want to avoid some rather uncomfortable situations when guests drop by, there are some noteworthy guidelines.

Personally speaking, you drink and eat whatever food and wine combinations you may happen to individually prefer. However, the complications arise when company comes by. Not everyone is wild about mustard on their strawberries or dills with their Torte. We all have our weird little taste habits, but, we shouldn't force them on our unsuspecting visitors; they may not think they're cute.

Besides, certain food and wine combinations almost seem meant for one another. They go together like coffee and cream, cake and icing, kids and mischief. Some very general matches worth remembering are:

Soups	· Medium sweet Sherry or Madeira
Seafoods	· Dry to semi-sweet white wines · dry Rosés
Poultry, pork	· Dry whites; light reds; dry Rosés
Beef	· Robust, full-bodied reds
Lamb	· Light reds, elegant whites
Fruits	· Sweet or semi-sweet whites; champagne
Desserts	· Sweet whites; demi-sec champagne, sweet crackling Rosés
Cheeses	· Dry whites with subtle and light-flavoured cheeses; full-bodied reds with stronger more full-flavoured types

One hint · if in doubt, don't order a Rosé. Because Rosé looks like it's half red and half white, that doesn't make it the ideal compromise. Rosés offend many foods and some people. Champagne is the only wine that seems to universally compliment most foods. But Champagne can be a little expensive and even out of place at the corner pizzeria; so it pays to know some of the basic food and wine partnerships.

Q. What wines go best with cheese?

A. Both cheese and wine are quite fickle · they've been known to switch partners on a number of occasions.

Cheese and Wine

The list of different cheeses, wines and their various combinations would take up most of this book. So we're stuck again with some gross generalities for the time being, at least.

The rule of thumb, if you trust rules of thumb, is the lighter flavoured the cheese, the lighter the wine. But avoid choosing rosés simply because they seem to be a happy medium. Nothing, always goes with everything · except nothing · and then only on certain occasions. Huh?? Anyway . . . Rosés go with some cheeses like ketchup goes with peaches. You might try these matches if you're so inclined. If not, oh well!

Havarti Edam Tilsit Gouda	Light reds Dry whites Dry rosés
Brie Camembert Swiss	Rieslings Anjou Rosés Bordeaux
Cheddar Roquefort Bleu Gorganjola	Barolos Traminers Burgundies Rhones

If your thumb doesn't fit these rules, experiment for yourself, but keep these guidelines in mind when serving guests. They may have a different size thumb.

Q. What wine is best to serve with Hors d'oeuvres?

A. If there were only one type of hors d'oeuvre, I could suggest only one type of wine. But there isn't, so I can't.

Hors d'Oeuvres

Hors d'oeuvres come in as many different sizes, shapes and descriptions as winter colds. The wines that go hand in hand with this prelude to the main course are just as varied.

However, a few clues might help to avoid some of the obvious disasters. One hint we might take rather seriously is to avoid serving any wine, white or red, sweet or dry with canapés or hors d'oeuvres made with vinegar. The conflict could start the meal on a sour note and it may never get back in tune.

Mindful of the general rule of thumb, light wines to be served before heavy, hors d'oeuvres seem to make friends best when served with white wines, especially those that tend to the sweeter side · but definitely not dessert wines.

The wines of the Loire Valley of France have a definite affinity for hors d'oeuvres. Both Anjou Rosés and Anjou Blancs make excellent choices, still or crackling. White Saumurs from the Loire are, too, among the best selections.

Spicy Traminers from Alsace or California are also delightful companions. But never let it be said we show ethnic bias · German Hocks and Moselles can be served with confidence. Rieslings from British Columbia are also proving to be noteworthy companions.

And if your pocketbook has survived reasonably the shock of inflation, and something of a dry wine is more to your liking, try a Pouilly Fuissé or a Chablis.

But if the choices are too infinite and decisions too wearisome, forget the hors d'oeuvres and serve the wine. They may never be missed.

Q. Which wine goes best with seafoods?

A. After spending your life in a lake or an ocean, it's hardly likely you'd be satisfied with any one single wine. And no self-respecting fish I know, is.

Seafoods

Again, we want to make some suggestions, but we don't want to sound dictatorial. For as soon as we indicate that one seafood goes better with a particular type of wine, the fish may change his mind and switch brands.

But just on the off chance we might hit the right combination why not try some of these partnerships.

Smoked Fish	· dry sherries or dry madeira
Oysters	· dry white Graves or Chablis
Clams	· Muscadet or Pouilly-Fuissé
Shrimps	· Rieslings
Lobster	· Champagne
Salt Water Fish	· Montrachet or Pouilly-Fumé
Fresh Water Fish	· Rieslings or dry Rosés
Chowders, Soups	· dry sherries, Traminers, Muscats

Most of these suggestions can be interchanged with little disappointment.

In case you want to put some of this into practical application try your next Perch or Trout served in this manner. It's an elegant inflation fighter.

Perch in Riesling

Ingredients:

4 fresh perch filleted (or 2 small cleaned trout) · 1-1/4 cups of milk · 2 tbsps. flour · 2 tbsps. butter · one half cup of Riesling wine · one cup sour cream · 2 egg yolks · salt · dried chervil · chopped parsley · pepper · ground nutmeg (all spices to taste, yours that is).

Dip fish in milk and dredge in the flour. Sauté in butter (15 minutes on each side) until golden brown. Remove the fish to a serving platter and keep warm. To the frying pan add the wine and sour cream. Stir well and add egg yolks and stir again. Simmer this sauce and reduce to approximately one cup. Add seasonings, stir until smooth. Pour over fish and serve.

Just to keep the fish happy, serve with a chilled bottle of the same Riesling.

Q. What do you need to know before you start to cook with wine?

A. A good brand of soda and a safe hiding place.

Cooking With Wine

Cooking with wine can elevate the ordinary to ambrosia. But it can also turn you against the grape for the rest of your life.

Serving wine and food together takes some forethought and an understanding of both food and wine. **Cooking** with wine demands even more care and attention.

You have to be cautious that the wine you choose for that special recipe is a wine that will compliment it. The general guidelines for **serving** wine with food are essentially applicable for **cooking** with wine. But of greater value is understanding how that wine reacts during the cooking process. After all, if you sat in a hot pot or an oven for a few hours, your disposition would likely be altered somewhat, too.

To understand what happens to the wine when it undergoes any cooking process, lace up your apron and join me in this little experiment. First, select the wine you think will go well with what you want to prepare. Open and pour yourself one or two ounces. Now taste it (interesting already, isn't it?). Now take another couple of ounces and simmer gently for a few minutes. Remove from the heat, cool and taste. By tasting, compare with the uncooked wine - note the differences?

Immediately you will sense, all the alcohol has been eliminated. And the fragrance of the wine has altered considerably. Now take another two ounces and cook gently for several hours. Cool, taste and compare with the uncooked wine and then that which was simmered for only a few minutes.

Again, you will notice a further transformation. In some ways you will now begin to appreciate what happens to the wine in your recipe. There is much more, but we've taken the first step in learning how to cook confidently with wine. The rest of the bottle is your reward for a hard day of experimenting.

Q. What is the difference between regular wine and cooking wine?

A. The same as the difference between regular cream and cooking cream - there isn't any!

Chapter IX

Cooking Wines?

The very expression "Cooking Wine" should be outlawed. The term itself seems to suggest a number of equally questionable and dastardly alternatives.

Is a **cooking wine** somehow not fit to drink? Does it have singularly unique qualities better suited to the kitchen? Does it impart some special additive to the food? The answer to each of these absurd questions is, of course, an emphatic NO!

If a wine is not fit to drink it's not fit to cook with either. Albeit, the pendulum can swing too far in the opposite direction. Those who insist upon using truly **great** wines in the kitchen have more imagination on their tongues than tastebuds. This can be a waste of money and wine. A happy medium is far better.

Some wines, of course, by their inherent qualities are more adaptable to certain foods. This takes experience and information to ascertain.

It's often asked, if you keep the remnants of an opened bottle in the fridge for a few days can you still cook with it? Some who are more oriented to the kitchen than the wine cellar answer, no, the wine will normally have turned to acidy to use. But such is not the case.

The increased acidity can be an asset to cooking. For example, if you prepare the same dish separately with Sherry, Madeira and Marsala - Madeira will win the taste contest on the majority of occasions. More often the reason will be the higher acid levels in Madeira. French chefs have known this for some time, that's why so many of their creations are 'a Madere.' They leave Sherry to the Spanish and Marsala to the Italians.

Q. What is the correct way to prepare the famous dish "Coq au vin"?

A. After quickly checking four of the world's great cooking reference volumes, and getting four different recipes, I'll pass on the right one - mine.

Coq au Vin

Actually, **coq au vin** is quite simple to prepare but is an elegant and quick dish when unexpected guests arrive. Each of the four renowned cooking authorities I checked, including Larousse Gastronomique, had only minor variances in their recipes.

The old, classic way of thickening the sauce was with chicken blood and a veal stock (as many restaurants in France still do). But for those of less sanguinary nature and who just don't happen to keep veal stock on hand, there are other methods of thickening the sauce which, are easier and in my opinion better anyway:

Cut a plump young chicken into 6 pieces. In a heavy deep skillet or casserole dish brown in 2 tbsps. of butter, 3 slices of diced bacon, 6 very small onions, 8 oz. of sliced mushrooms. When browned add one crushed garlic clove, the chicken pieces, basil to taste and sauté on a lively heat for 4-5 minutes. Remove the lid and skim off the fat. Add 1-2 ozs. of warmed brandy and flame. When the flame dies out add 10 ozs. of dry red table wine (to save some pennies try an Italian Valpolicella, Chianti or Bardolino) with lid off simmer for 15-20 minutes. Remove chicken to serving dish. Thicken remaining liquid with a 'beurre manie' (equal parts of soft butter and flour mixed well together) to desired consistency. Pour over chicken, garnish and serve.

As a late night tantalizer, serve with garlic bread, cool cucumber slices and a bottle of the same wine used in the recipe. Where's the kitchen?

Q.   What wine is best to serve with Coquille St. Jacques?

A.   Before you serve it you have to make it - that's half the joy.

Les Coquilles St. Jacques

Recipes for Coquilles St. Jacques are as numerous as chefs. I like this one best - after all it's mine.

Thoroughly wash 1 lb. of scallops. In a small pot bring to a simmer 8-10 ounces of Muscadet wine from the Loire Valley of France (if

Chapter IX

Muscadet is not available a dry Italian white like Soave will do). Place the scallops in the simmering wine and boil gently for 6-8 minutes. Remove and cut the scallops into pieces (approx. 1/2 inch). Reserve the wine.

Melt 2 tbsps. of butter in a skillet and when golden brown add 2 tbsps. of flour. Cook very slowly until the mixture takes on a nutty fragrance, but do not let it brown. Reserve this mixture.

Now in another skillet melt 1 tbsp. of butter, add a dash or two of Worcestershire sauce and sauté approximately 1/4 cup of finely chopped onions (spanish preferably) and about 1/2 lb. of sliced mushrooms. Sauté until onions become transparent. Add basil and salt to taste. Now add the warm wine to your "roux" (the flour and butter) mix and add to the onions and mushrooms. As you finally add the scallops blend in 8 ounces of heavy (whipping) cream and simmer complete mixture for 2 or 3 minutes. Portion the mixture into Coquilles Shells (shallow meat pie tins can substitute). Ten minutes before you serve your dish sprinkle with fresh fine bread crumbs, dot with butter and place under the broiler until they become golden. Et Voila!

Oh yes, serve with a chilled bottle of Muscadet or the wine you chose to use in the recipe.

Q. Which wine is best to cook chicken in?

A. We could make all kinds of suggestions, but in the end it's up to the chicken. And they enjoy a little variety, too.

Chickens and Wine

Chicken can be the backbone, although they don't enjoy the distinction, of an unlimited variety of succulent main courses. And both red and white table wines can be employed to create distinctive results.

The classic "Coq au vin" uses a light red wine (inexpensive Italian reds such as Bardolino and Valpolicella are ideal). But don't conclude too hastily that reds are always superior. That's bound to alienate a few chickens that definitely prefer whites.

If you have a little adventure in your heart, a spare bottle of Riesling and a few stray chicken breasts, try this:

Remove the skin from two chicken breasts. De-bone and separate the four double fillets. With a bottle or a plate, flatten the breasts slightly, without breaking too much of the meat fibre. Dredge in diluted egg white and fine bread crumbs. In an oven to stove-top pan, sauté the breasts in butter (approximately 3 minutes each side). Add three ounces of white wine (any Riesling) and place in an oven at 325 deg. for 15 minutes. Every 15 minutes add two ounces of wine and baste in its own juices. Repeat until the chicken is done (approx. 45 minutes). Remove the breasts from the pan and keep warm.

Add 1 tbsp. of flour to the pan juices and make a light roux on top of the stove. Add more flour if needed. Cook well but do not brown. When it gives off a nutty fragrance add rich cream to make a sauce of the consistency you individually prefer. Add a touch of basil and a half pound of sliced mushrooms that have already been sautéed in butter. Pour the sauce over the chicken, garnish as you may prefer and serve; knowing full well that the chicken went with a smile on its beak.

Serve with a chilled bottle of the wine you used in cooking.

Q. I enjoy German white wines and late-evening snacks - any suggestions?

A. Find a good German restaurant that stays open late!

Late-Evening Dining

If you'll excuse the flip response - I assume you meant what recipes might I have that would meet these circumstances. And I must admit I'm a fan of both of the above. And nothing is more enjoyable when you want to entertain a few close friends than to invite them, not for dinner but for late-evening snacks and wine.

And since your favorite wines are German - try this two-course "mini-meal". Main course: **Shrimps in White Wine.** Dessert: **Sweet Toast.**

Chapter IX

Shrimps in White Wine

Ingredients: 1-1/2 lbs. shelled, deveined jumbo shrimps · 1 oz. lemon juice · 1 tsp. sweet basil · small clove crushed garlic · salt and pepper to taste · 8 oz. German white wine. Place all ingredients in a shallow dish and marinate in refrigerator for at least 2 hours. (4-6 hours if you have the time). Separate shrimps and sauté in 2 tbsps. of butter for 8-10 minutes. Remove shrimp to serving dish. Pour marinade into same skillet on high heat and reduce volume to about 1/3. Pour over shrimps. Garnish with parsley. Serve over toast. Serves 4

Sweet Toast

Ingredients: 4 ozs. German White Wine · 1 egg · 2 ozs. granulated sugar · 1/2 tsp. vanilla extract · 4 pieces of thickly-sliced French or Italian style bread (approx. 3/4" thick). Beat wine, egg, sugar and vanilla together. Dredge bread slices in mixture and sauté in sweet butter until golden brown on both sides. Serve hot, sprinkled with confectioner's sugar or strawberry preserves and whipped cream. Serves 4.

Serve chilled bottles of the same wine.

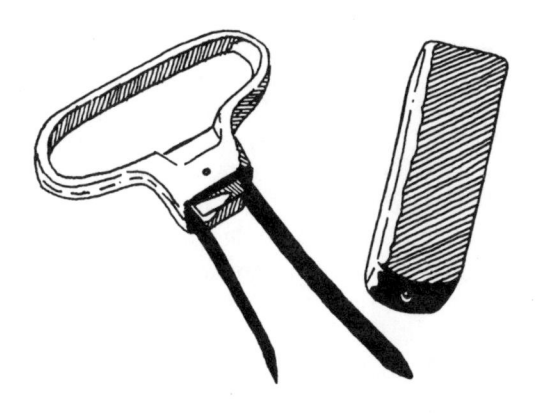

Chapter X

Wine and Health

Q. Is there any nutritional or medicinal value to wine?

A. Yes and yes. Wine is one alcoholic beverage that can be justified on grounds other than as a producer of revenue for government coffers.

To Your Health . . .

According to Louis Pasteur, "Wine is the healthiest and most hygenic drink there is." But Louis, being French and all, might have been slightly biased, so we'd be wise to consider a little more evidence.

There are a number of valid reasons you can give your spouse when bringing home a goodly supply of this "grape juice for grown-ups." First, wine is not just another alcoholic drink, but a very complex, living substance. So far, science has identified nearly 400 constituents that make up wine . . . and they're still discovering.

Next to blood, and perhaps milk, wine is the most complex biological liquid known to man. And wine offers some nutritional elements not found in milk. Wine contains yeasts, enzymes, vitamins (from many groups), minerals, sugars, glycerol, organic acids, proteins, alcohols and iron. In fact, for women, wine is an excellent and a natural source of usable iron. Need I say more, ladies?

Medicinally, wine is becoming more appreciated every year.

Recent medical research in Italy, France and California indicates that wine taken with meals not only inhibits but **may** even totally curtail cholesterol accumulation. Some researchers claim that arteriosclerotic vascular disease (heart disease) could be cut in half in North America if we all got into the habit of drinking moderate amounts of wine with our meals. It's already been flatly stated by some authorities that people who drink wine in moderation live longer than either abstainers or those who are immoderate drinkers.

Wine is also the oldest, most natural and effective sedative available. Geriatric patients increasingly enjoy wine as part of a daily prescribed regimine. A glass of wine before retiring could put sleeping pill manufacturers out of business.

These are but a few of the benefits that wine, taken in moderation, offers. Happily more and more doctors are becoming aware of its value. What a prescription . . . ONE BOTTLE OF BORDEAUX - 3-4 OUNCES, FOUR TIMES DAILY.

Q. In one of your articles you noted the value of wine from a health standpoint. Are our native Canadian wines as good for you as European wines?

A. Just ask any self-respecting Canadian grape - he'll answer, certainly!

"Good Health To You"

We could safely state, that only occasionally does the **wine-making** quality of a grape bear a relationship to its medicinal or nutritive value. Some species of grapes that produces wines of questionable character can be, generally speaking, as 'good for you' as the ones used to vint the most famed Chateau wines of France.

But again, occasionally certain red wines will be superior to other red wines, if you were to consider them for a specific ailment. And generally speaking most reds are superior to white wines. Different varieties of red or blue grapes pass on a varied number of beneficial elements to their wines. Age isn't much of a factor either, as their value for considerable lengths of time.

Native Canadian grapes, although of a totally different species when compared to European breeds, seem every bit as good from the nutritive and medicinal viewpoint. However, making high quality wines from them is a totally different matter.

So, if you are drinking wine for that proverbial **medicinal** reason or just plain good health, the brand will not be all that significant. Specific wines can be better for specific ailments though. There is however, one practice that can for some, detract from a wine's value. The addition of cane sugar.

Yet, this is not a problem with dry table wines. Even those producers who do add sugar to table wines usually do so during the fermentation period whereupon the sugar is completely converted into alcohol. It does not show up as sweetness or calorically affect the consumer in any way. Only when sugar is used to sweeten wines, like cheap Ports and Sherries, is it not beneficial.

So some Canadian-made dry red table wines (try the ones with corks as closures instead of those with screw caps) have as much going for them, healthwise, as any in the world.

Q. Quite to my surprise and delight, my doctor, recently suggested I take a little wine each day for a certain medical condition I have. I'm curious to know - is this something new, a doctor prescribing wine?

A. Indeed not! Especially if your condition is thirst. For that, it's always been an ideal remedy.

Medicinal Wine

The era of prohibition and the vociferous energy of North American temperance groups did much to remove wine from public favour. And, it all but disappeared from the medical profession in the decades immediately following. And all this despite wine having been used for thousands of years as a proven medical tool of considerable value.

The almost spastic rejection by the scientific community of the

40's and 50's of anything considered a **home** remedy pushed wine further into the background. With giant strides being made in modern medical research, resulting in a parade of **wonder** drugs, lowly wine was all but medically forgotten - until recently.

The falacy that wine's only redeeming quality lies in its alcohol content has now been successfully discredited. Yet, the vast majority of doctors are still not aware of the findings of recent wine research, sufficient to prescribe it. So, your doctor displays an admirable picture of being up-to-date.

More and more one finds members of the medical profession prescribing wine for a growing list of ailments. Among its nearly 400 known constituents wine consists of vitamins, minerals, alcohols, sugars, acids, tannins and trace elements galore.

When someone lifts a glass of wine and says "To your health", the phrase should be considered more practical than traditional. Despite our conditioned response to medicine's tasting bad - wine is one prescription few of us mind getting filled. I wonder if the Liquor Control Board accepts Blue Cross?

Q. In a recent article you intimated Wine was beneficial for certain ailments? As a doctor I'm curious to know specifically which ailments?

A. Thirst. Good taste. Loss of your sense of humour. And a number of more serious ailments.

Medicinal Wine - Part II

Modern scientific investigators have demonstrated that wine is medically beneficially in a number of very significant ways. The Massachusetts Department of Public Health recently stated: "the medical uses of wine are on the increase as many physicians are taking a second look at its restorative qualities as aids to the sick and infirmed. In sipping a glass of wine, evidence appears . . . we give a lift to our general health and well-being."

Ingredients (other than alcohol) are responsible for wines' success in combating certain infectious diseases. Researchers in France and California have discovered that the anthocynin pigments in wine have an antibiotic effect, working especially against intestinal bacteria such as salmonella bacilli (a frequent cause of food poisoning) and staphylococcus strains. Because of this antibacterial quality, wine is more often being recommended in the treatment of intestinal colic, colitis, constipation, diarrhea and a number of other infections of the gastrointestinal tract.

As well, wine aids the digestion because its degree of acidity resembles the natural acidity of the stomach more closely than any other beverage. Especially is this important to elderly patients because it increases the flow of digestive juices and acts as both a diaphoretic and a diuretic - functions which are apt to be defective in later years.

The sense of well-being derived from wine, and its anesthetic quality originates from more than its alcohol content. An ethyl ester of gamma-hydroxybutyric acid, together with its lactone form gamma-butyrolactone (a recognized safe and effective anaesthetic) and ellagic acid (a known tranquilizer) are both present in wine.

These are but a few of wines' medicinal advantages. Dr. S.P. Lucia, M.D., D.Sc. of the University of California well phrased it when he said, "If wine were discovered today, it would rightly be considered the best wonder drug of all." And this is only the tip of the medical iceberg where wine is concerned.

A bottle of Burgundy, please!

Q. Can you drink wine on a diet?

A. It all depends upon what you're trying to lose - a few pounds or your sense of taste.

Wine and Your Diet

There's no doubt wine has calories, and sweet wines do have more calories than dry wines (approximately 40-50 calories per ounce for sweet wines compared to 20-25 calories per ounce for dry wines). However, before you ban wines from your next diet consider this: dry wines used in cooking lose 85% of their caloric content.

Also, calories from wine seem to react somewhat differently in the body than do food calories. Wine-alcohol calories are not **empty** calories. Wine yields almost total energy. It significantly enhances the absorption of nutrients from the diet. Wine included in a diet causes people to naturally tend towards a reduction in carbohydrate intake.

If equivalent wine calories are substituted for an equal amount of food calories, it has been demonstrated that there is an increase in the rate of weight loss (almost twice the rate). Wine, as a bonus, also puts the user in a more amicable frame of mind to face the rigors of dieting. I can attest to this personally.

On crash diets, proper nutrition is always of concern. Wine contains vitamins and all major minerals so can be a desirable compliment to such a regimen. It can also help you keep your mind off your arch enemy - food. Using wine before bedtime reduces insomnia thusly the temptation for a late-night raid on the refrigerator.

On low carbohydrate-high protein diets, cholesterol becomes a major consideration and danger. But wine is proving to be a significant agent in preventing cholesterol deposits in the blood vessels. This too makes it the dieter's friend.

To relieve the boredom of the same old diet foods "The Wine Diet Cookbook" by Dr. Lucia and Emily Chase from Longmans can be of indispensible aid in maintaining your sense of taste even under diet conditions.

Q. You mentioned before that wine can be used when you are on a diet. Any hints?

A. As one inextricably engaged in the battle of the bulge, I am able to pass on some tips from personal experience.

The Wine War Against Weight

Wine as a beverage can be drunk in moderation on most diets. To help you in assessing how much, here is a table for wine calories.

Red table wines · 20-25 calories per ounce

White table wines	· 22-25 calories per ounce
Rosés	· 22-24 calories per ounce
Dry Sherries	· 35-40 calories per ounce
Sweet Ports and Sherries	· 45-50 calories per ounce

Much to the nibbler's delight, wines lose from 75 to 90 percent of their calories when cooked. So on with the apron.

One valuable hint - don't drink your wine before the meal. It'll only sharpen your appetite. Save it for the meal - eat slowly - and you'll find you need less food to be satisfied.

Here is one of my favourite dishes for dieting in style.

Veal with Mushrooms

Ingredients: 1 lb. of veal steak, 1/2 lb. fresh mushrooms, flour, 1 tbsp. diet margarine, 1 clove of fresh garlic. Spices: salt, pepper, thyme and marjoram, Worcestershire sauce, chopped parsley, 4 oz. of dry white table wine.

Directions: Pound the veal to about 1/4" thickness. Dredge both sides in flour. Cut into serving pieces. Slice mushrooms. Melt margarine in a skillet, add chopped or pressed garlic clove and cook for 2 minutes. Brown veal on both sides over medium heat. Add spices to taste. Add Worcestershire sauce to taste. Add mushrooms and wine, cover and simmer gently for 40-45 minutes. To keep the sauce a desirable consistency you can add as needed a mixture of 1/2 water and 1/2 wine. Sprinkle with parsley and serve. (Serves three at about 275 calories per serving.) With 4 oz. of the same wine and an appropriate salad, here's a gourmet treat for about 550 calories in all. What a way to lose!

Chapter XI

Canada

Q. How long have they been making wine in Canada?

A. To some Europeans, we never have. But historically our vintages go back to about the middle 1600's.

Canadian Wine History

Around 1636 there are records that make reference to some Jesuit priests in Quebec making wine from our native Canadian grape varieties. The results seemed at least palatable and it appears they continued making more each year after.

For some strange reason Canadian wine history goes mysteriously silent for almost two hundred years and the next historical account, in 1811, refers to wines being made by a transplanted German army corporal, Johann Schiller. Apparently, he too decided to try the local vines that grew naturally around Cooksville. And naturally he wasn't beyond charging a 'schilling' or two for those who wanted to purchase the odd jug. At any rate, he's referred to by some in the Canadian wine industry as the "father of Canadian winemakers."

The first man known to actually cultivate grapes on a commercial basis seems to have been a chap named Porter Adams around the year 1857. By the mid-1860's dozens of small family wineries had sprouted up mainly in parts of Southwestern Ontario.

These smaller operations were eventually absorbed into larger ones, simply went out of business or were run out of town by local consumers who may not have appreciated their wine-making talents. And today what's left are mostly large corporate entities that have survived these years, including prohibition and what it wrought for the Canadian wine industry - a rotten reputation they've been trying to live down ever since.

Q. Wasn't there some Canadian discovery which was supposed to take all the "foxy" taste out of Canadian wines?

A. Yes! It was called European grapes. (Not really).

Methyl Anthranilate

The chemical substance which so profoundly identifies wines made from native North American grapes (species Vitis Labrusca) has been identified as METHYL ANTHRANILATE. This chemical, inherent in the grape skins is responsible for imparting to Canadian wines the 'foxy' taste and aroma which has sent so many wine lovers running to Imported labels.

After a number of years researching ways to rid out native grapes of this characteristic, thus ridding Concord and its ilk of the 'fox' stigma, scientists at the Horticultural Research Station in Vineland, Ontario announced a cure in 1973.

Actually it is a take-off on the way Beaujolais wine is made in France - carbonic maseration. Enough of the fifty cent words, you say! In the average grape lovers' lingo - the Beaujolais process finds grapes in tanks or vats, being crushed by their own weight, grapes piled on grapes, not by large mechanical presses. Being enclosed in these containers a carbon-dioxide atmosphere develops and what wine-makers call inter-cellular fermentation.

All this has the end result of imparting to the wine a soft, round taste with a characteristic lack of the usual greenness and harshness usually associated with young wines. Being able to be drunk so young while being so ready to drink has made Beaujolais one of the best

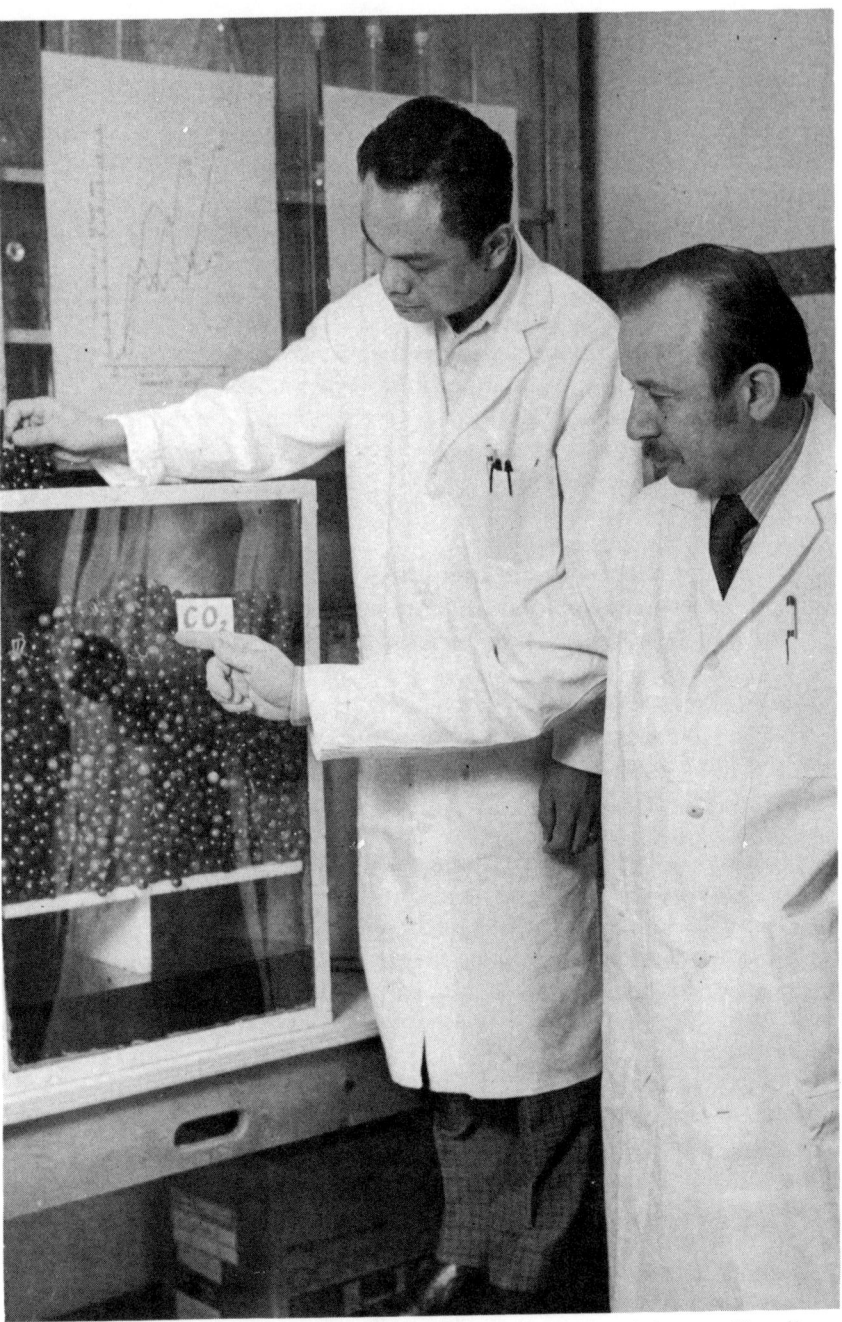

Dr. Fuleki and assistant describe basic procedure to reduce infamous "foxy" character of native Canadian vines.

known wines in the world.

Now apply this thinking to our Concords, only put the fresh uncrushed grapes in sealed tanks, pump out the oxygen and add carbon dioxide. This in a simple way describes our so-called cure. Wines from this process, even though pure North American in heritage are indeed distinguished from their previous 'foxy' state.

Improved? Yes! Transformed? No! You can still detect the 'fox'. Yet, if this process is applied to the new batch of hybrids coming out, it could indeed be a big step forward. A cure? Hardly! A shot in the arm? By all means.

Q. I've heard that all the grape vines in Europe were once destroyed by a plant disease and they all had to be replaced by North American vines. Is this actually true?

A. Yes and no. If totally true I imagine it would be the answer to a life-long prayer for some Canadian wine producers; while to European winemakers it's something they would just rather not talk about.

Phylloxera Vastatrix

It's a mean sounding name and it couldn't be more appropriate to the little insect or plant louse that it identifies. For the phylloxera louse is the most devastating of all the enemies of the vine. Just whisper the word and the hearts of European winemakers go into fibrilation.

It's quite reasonable to assume that this little louse existed in the Eastern United States for several milleniums of time. But the native North American species of grapes had developed an immunity to it, partially because of their more substantial and tougher root stocks. Not so with the European Vinifera variety of grapes.

Our local louse seemingly made its way to Europe via some cuttings sent there for research purposes, around 1860. However, in a span of less than twenty years this disease had devastated virtually all of the vines in Europe; some two and one half million acres of vineyards in France alone. There's still some suspicion as

Chapter XI

to whether this occurred at the hands of some jealous North American winemaker (I'm only kidding, so please no nasty letters from the Canadian Wine Institute). But whatever, it was essentially total in its annihilation of the European wine industry.

Despite valiant efforts to find a cure all remedies failed, except for isolated pockets. But in the nick of time, a savior did appear - and from the same place the disease originated. North American rootstocks which were highly resistant to the disease were transplanted to the troubled vineyards. European cuttings were grafted to these American rootstocks and Europe was back in the wine business. So, today virtually all European grapes are grown on North American-type rootstocks. The grapes remain European but the roots are offsprings from North America.

Debate still continues over whether European wines prior to this disaster were better than those today, grafted on our rootstocks. Though the issue can never be totally resolved it appears recent vintages are every bit as good as they ever were.

Q. Where do Canadians stand as world winedrinkers?

A. Somewhere, away down the line - but we're moving up fast. In the trade we're known as a "future contender."

Wine Consumption

For generations Canadians have felt it somewhat decadent to even have a bottle of wine **with** their meal. But gradually this stigma has eroded and wine has become a respectable guest at the dinner table.

By the early 1960's we were consuming about one half gallon of this adult grape juice, per person per year. When the late sixties arrived we were getting close to .7 gallons of wine per capita. The explosion was just starting. Then by 1973 the full impact of the movement to the vineyards was being felt, because we had gone over the full gallon mark per person. This meant, in less than five years, we had doubled our national consumption of wine. And that's just a start. Forecasts for the future show a continual growth in our

Whether it's California's Sonoma Valley (above) or the vines of Alsace (below) many of the finer wine regions bear striking resemblances in topography.

rate of consumption, some experts claiming we will quadruple our individual consumption rate before 1990.

But wait a minute! Before you get the impression we've turned into a nation of instant winos or you start to organize your own chapter of A.A., consider what some other countries are doing.

At the head of the list for national consumption rates are both France and Italy. They consume 29-30 gallons of wine per person each year - about 20 times our paltry rate. To suggest we have room for growth is the proverbial understatement. We're still in the minors in comparison.

Canadians spend more than two hundred million dollars a year on wine. This might seem a fantastic sum yet it is a small fraction of what we spend on junk foods and drinks, such as soda pop and candy bars. It would be far better for our national health if we exchanged these soft drinks for something a bit harder. Not too hard, mind you.

Q. Why can you buy the same wine for so much less in the United States than in Canada?

A. Because the price is lower! But not always for legitimate reasons.

Price Comparisons

There are a number of reasons why prices for imported wine in Canada tend to be higher, on occasion, than for the same imported wine in parts of the United States. But this is not always the case. Some states, 18 to be precise, sell liquor and wine only through government outlets, as is done in Canada. Their prices are as high or higher for some imports than ours.

The other 32 states operate under the private enterprise arrangement. And it is in these states that one usually finds some price discrepancies or just plain bargains.

Most importantly, though, private enterprise distribution channels are also the chief target for fraudulent wines (cheap wines bearing more expensive, well-known labels). There's no doubt, this type of fraudulent import can be bought for less than the real thing in Canada. For, such dishonest wines are not available here because of the stiff screening processes imposed by the Liquor Boards. They weed out such frauds before they ever reach the Canadian consumer.

But, even when comparing prices for many imports nose to nose with an American private retailer our prices don't fare badly for popular brand names. Compare the following with a N.Y. state cut-rate store, priced in October, 1975.

	Ontario	N.Y.	Quebec
Mateus Rosé	$2.65	$3.19	$2.55
Pinot Noir (Lichine)	3.90	3.49	3.50
Egri Bikaver (Hungary)	2.35	3.69	2.65
Mouton Cadet	4.15	3.99	3.65
Chianti Riserva Ducale	4.05	4.95	4.00

There are a variety of other reasons why some of the more expensive imported wines often sell in the U.S. for a fraction of the Canadian price . . . reasons such as, wine futures, dumping due to over-buying in past years, holding wines too long . . . are just a few.

Although, prices for imported wines tend to be higher on our side of the border so does the integrity of the products.

Q. I've heard the expression "Pop wine" used on several occasions. What does it mean?

A. The real question is - which is it? Pop or wine?

Pop Wine

The simplest and most expedient way to define "pop wine" is that they are wines containing a maximum of 7% alcohol by volume. This is about half of normal table wines which range from 9-14% alcohol.

Names such as Baby Duck, Cold Turkey, Free Spirit, Baby

Chapter XI

Duckling, Canada Duck, Fuddle Duck, Hot Goose, Sno Bird are but a few of such wines on the market today.

If we want to be somewhat more descriptive, **pop wine** is made from inferior grapes, is artificially carbonated (as is soda pop), needs more preservatives, is bulk produced, and lacks the benefit of ageing. Not to mention less alcohol.

Yet, they've captured an enviable chunk of the Canadian wine market (18%). Canada's best selling wine is Andres' Baby Duck, a 'pop wine'. The fad first struck in the United States. However, it is in its death throes there, today. Canada soon followed the fad but its fate here promises to be no finer despite being at its peak now.

As a wine **pop wine** is not worthy of an evaluation of its status in the wine world. Nor, do I believe its producers ever intended it to be so judged.

Pop wines find their greater number of devotees among the younger set. And more basically, those who are just beginning to explore the world of wine. Herein, perhaps, lies its singular merit as a wine · a bridge between the novice and the seasoned wine drinker.

So, pop or wine? A little of both. And at best, an introduction to better wines ahead.

Q.   Why are "POP" wines so popular today?

A.   If you'll excuse the alliteration, three reasons · price, packaging and plenty.

Why Pop Wines?

The PLENTY comes from an abundance of poorer wine grapes from the Labrusca grape species (Concord for example) grown in the Niagara region. Although, there is a gradual move afoot to replace these native grapes with crossbreeds of European extraction and pure European varieties, both making superior wines, it all takes time. Currently about 27% of the domestic grape harvest is made up of hybrids and pure European types.

So, the booming popularity of **POP** wines was a boon to Canadian producers. They have a breathing spell and an outlet for these poorer grapes.

PRICE is always a factor in selling any product. And the manufacturers of POP wine well knew that if you made a wine which had 7% alcohol, or less, a great savings could be had on the taxes levied on wine.

Sparkling wines over 7% alcohol, such as Champagne, are unjustly saddled with an excise tax of $2.95 per gallon - about 60¢ a bottle. But with 7% alcohol, or below, they are charged less than 10¢ per bottle. This disparity would reflect well over $1.00 difference on a bottle of wine selling at $3.50 to $4.00. So, there was no guessing when they decided to make POP wine 7% alcohol by volume.

Add to this the PACKAGING - 'noble' looking labels, gold foil around the neck, caps that 'pop' off, and you create the illusion of a more expensive wine. So, consumers and producers of such wines as Baby Duck, Barnee, Cold Duckling, Canada Duck, Jolly Friar, Judge Frost, Cold Turkey, Golden Goose and many others, take a certain delight in these wines. 'Good taste alone' may not recommend them, but they sure do sell.

Q. I've heard our wine industry uses them, but just what are HYBRID grapes?

A. Birds do it, bees do it, even grapes do it . . . have offspring, that is.

Hybrids

The purpose of hybridizing or cross-breeding grape species is to develop an offspring with more desirable characteristics . . . the fond hope of many a parent.

Our Canadian climate and soil conditions demand that if a species of grapes is going to survive and produce economically it must be hardy, prolific and highly disease resistant. Our native Labrusca grapes more than fill the bill in this respect. But alas, the unique taste it imparts to its wines is becoming less acceptable to the general Canadian wine public. The more subtle qualities of the European Vinifera grapes are filling this demand in the manner of soaring imported wine sales.

The obvious reaction and solution to this problem might seem to be, simply cultivate and vint wines from European grapes right here. However, that's tantamount to saying, just build a rocket and send it to the moon. For viniferas aren't passionately in love with our local climate, don't proliferate as well here as our Labruscas, and aren't as disease resistant.

Ah, ha! Hybrids, you say? Right! And some thirty years ago a programme to develop grapes by crossing European and American varieties was undertaken with some very interesting results. Results that could be called a ray of sunshine for the Canadian wine industry, not a full-fledged sunburst mind you, but nevertheless, definitely a ray.

Certain varieties of these hybrids have been chosen for use in major commercial production and have become available in enough quantity to be released to the public unblended with any pure native varieties. Names like Foch, Veeburg, Seibel, Chelois, de Chaunac and Verdelet are bound to become more familiar to Canadian wine drinkers. And although most of these hybrids were developed in Europe they have seemingly taken to Canadian vineyards like a beaver to water.

Q. Baco Noir, de Chaunac, Chelois and Marechal Foch are some new Canadian wines I've seen lately. Are they any good?

A. That all depends on who answers the question.

Canadian Varietals

Over 40 years ago some Canadian winemakers realized the growing importance of **table** wines and imported a number of crossbreeds. As well, they undertook to establish their own hybrid varieties of grapes. Their goal . . . to be able to produce dry table wines without that foxy, overly-grapey taste native to local vines.

Although a few of the Canadian-originated hybrids show promise, major successes are to be found primarily with the hybrids transplanted from Europe. Four or five predominate.

Baco Noir is actually Baco No. 1 developed by Maurice Baco, a French hybridizer. It is more full-bodied than the other hybrids but to date it lacks the finesse and breed to ever be considered a distinguished wine grape. It is palatable and priced well.

Chelois is another French hybrid success. Seibel 10878, as it's known in the trade, is at least fifth generation hybrid, having more than 17 different parents. It is one of the more refreshing of the hybrids on the market . . . not as full as Baco Noir but is eminently pleasant to drink. Its future is questionable, though.

de Chaunac too, is a Seibel Hybrid 9549, one of the most promising. Actually originates from 4 varieties of grapes Labrusca (North American), Vinifera (European), Rupestris and Riparia. It is light-bodied, a vin ordinaire. Sometimes erroneously compared to Beaujolais . . . there is really no comparison.

Marechal Foch is an Alsatian hybrid (Kuhlmann 188-2). Essentially a cross between the famous Pinot Noir and Gamay (Beaujolais) grapes. Wine made from these grapes grown in Canada bear little resemblance to their forerunners. Wine is earthy, fairly full, seems to age well.

Villard Noir another European Hybrid. Deep crimson in colour. Pronounced "foxy" character. A little too acidic. May age well. Overpriced.

Q. I've seen a new Canadian wine labelled "Chardonnay". Isn't this a French grape?

A. Yes, but it immigrated.

Canadian Chardonnay

Often called the Pinot Chardonnay, this grape is one of the leading candidates for "greatest white grape of the world award". Its vinuous offspring leads the wine-world's who's who list for white wines . . . Chablis, Montrachet, Pouilly-Fuisse and even Champagne.

Chapter XI

Its characteristic low yields have not made it all that enticing to North American vintners, who prefer a higher yield to acre ratio - it's more profitable. But alas, it has appeared in some Canadian vineyards in very limited quantities, on an experimental basis . . .

When sold in its varietal state (labelling by grape variety) it usually appears as 'Pinot Chardonnay'. More properly it should be labelled simply 'Chardonnay' as its relation to the true Pinot family (Pinot Noir, Pinot Blanc, etc.) is questionable.

And when buying a North American version of Chardonnay extra care is needed. You are advised to ask first - is it 100% Chardonnay? Established American and proposed Canadian definitions for varietal wines would allow for as much as 49% of another grape variety to be blended with it - while still calling it, in this case, Chardonnay. Other varietals are guilty of the same practice.

But Canadian wineries only appear to be folowing the lead of many other wine lands in allowing for this detestable practice. Unless labels truly define their contents it borders on outright fraud. Few other industries would be allowed such liberties. In an age of growing consumer awareness it would seem the trend should be in the opposite direction . . . but it isn't.

Generally the wine industry has led the way in 'truth in packaging' but in the case of Varietals it's fallen flat on its cork. Chardonnay is no exception.

To be assured you're getting a true Chardonnay, 100% of it, strangely enough, you have to go to a generic name such as a French Chablis or Montrachet, etc. Some vintners rightly claim that limited blending actually may improve the wine when compared to 100% of its variety . . . and they're right, it can. But then why not call it a blend? State it so on the label. Why hide behind the varietal name. The theory "only your little old winemaker knows for sure what's inside," is just not acceptable today.

Q. I recently purchased a bottle of wine called "GAMAY". A friend told me this is the same as a Beaujolais wine. Is this true?

A. No! But your friend was obviously in the same ball park, though. He just happened to strike out on this particular occasion.

Gamay - Beaujolais

'Gamay' is a variety of grape. It is one of an increasing number of wines being sold by the name of the grape (Varietal) as opposed to marketing wines by Generic names like Burgundy or Champagne.

In this particular instance, Gamay is indeed the same grape used in the production of Beaujolais wines. But that doesn't make all wines vinted from the Gamay a Beaujolais.

Something unique takes place when the Gamay grape is grown in the delimited district of Beaujolais in France. Experts universally recognize that this same Gamay grape when grown outside Beaujolais falls far short of reaching a similar quality. Soil, climate and the vines themselves come together in Beaujolais to create a unique offspring.

But just go outside this district, even in nearby parts of France itself and the quality drops significantly. A true Beaujolais wine is also made in a very different fashion. "Carbonic Maseration" is the term used to describe its special fermentation process. Imitators, even those who use the Gamay grape rarely use this special process and so the results are never the same.

Yet, the Gamay grape, wherever grown generally yields wines of a pleasing, noble nature. They have been transplanted to Canadian vineyards and appear to be doing well. Canadian producers have brought to market what they label as a "Gamay - Beaujolais".

It may have been more appropriate to label them simply - Gamay, which they truly are - for a Beaujolais they aren't. The vines imported may have been called "Gamay - Beaujolais" vines, but the wine produced isn't. But the continual poaching of European generic names remains part of Canadian wine producers' philosophy. Hopefully, our producers will some day be proud enough of their own wines to let them stand on their own merits and with their own names.

Chapter XII

France

Q. Is there any advantage when a wine is "estate" bottled?

A. If you are the estate owner, very probably, yes. If not, yes and no.

Estate Bottled

This question usually revolves around the wines of France. The famous expression, "mis en bouteille au Chateau" for example, indicates that the wine in question was produced and bottled right at the Chateau or the estate itself. This is a guarantee of authenticity. And although, usually only wines of finer quality are estate bottled it is however, no guarantee of that wine's status. Some very ordinary wines are estate bottled, too.

As well, a very noted wine shipper (négociant) may also be a vineyard owner (propriétaire). He may, on the one hand, produce estate bottled wines from his own vineyards. But, he may also select very fine crops from nearby growers who don't vint their own harvest. A good example of such is the house of Louis Jadot, one of the most famous in all France. The wines produced from his purchased grapes may be every bit as good as his own wines but it is not entitled to the distinction of being **estate bottled.**

This practice is no stranger to the Burgundian district of France

When the wine reaches the bottling line, whether it's California (above) or France's Champagne region (below) it all looks very much the same.

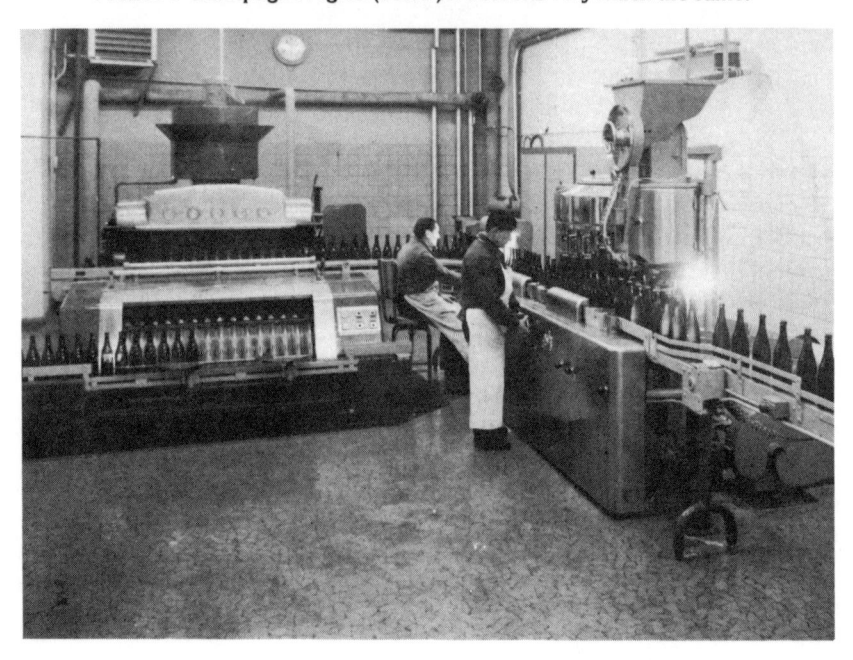

because there are so many very small vineyards. Too small to economically produce and bottle their own wine.

So, these grapes, that are selectively bought by such shippers, are then taken back to their estate, carefully vinted and bottled. The expression "mis en bouteille du Domaine" may appear on these labels and could still represent some of the finest wines in all of the world. But everything depends on the reputation of that shipper and the 'appellation' to which the wine is entitled.

But France is not alone in **estate bottling.** Germany, for years, has been very much involved, too. "Original Abfüllung" is the equivalent Teutonic expression. And each year more and more vineyard owners are beginning to bottle their own product. It is a welcomed move as far as consumer welfare is concerned. And to a lesser degree very limited amounts of California and Canadian wines are now being distinguished by this **estate bottled** designation.

Q. Does the term "Chateau" have any legitimate meaning on a wine label?

A. If you're not a wine drinker, "Chateau" is the French word for a country estate home. If you're French and do drink wine it means everything. But, if you are not French but still drink wine, it can mean a lot. Understand? Oh, well . . .

Chateau

As consumer militancy reaches new heights in this decade many consumer frauds have been unearthed. Frauds are those things we used to call 'commercial liberties', remember?

The taint of fraud has not passed over the vineyards of France without leaving a stain here and there. Yet French wine stature remains relatively intact despite the large media play on actual and alleged scandals.

The use of the word **Chateau** on a French wine label is strictly controlled by the French government. It can only appear on labels where an actual vineyard exists and can only be used by that particular vineyard owner.

This prevents devious wine merchants from buying up various wines from different districts and hawking them with a gilt-edged label as a Chateau wine. Yet it is still only a very relative indication to authenticity of origin.

Some French Chateaux are truly magnificent country estates that bottle wines of world renown. While other Chateau are not much more than a chicken coup in the middle of an acre and a half of grape vines. Yet, both can legally sport **Chateau** on their labels. And there are literally thousands of Chateaux in France.

So, Chateau merely means; the wine in that bottle comes solely from the designated vineyard and that particular vineyard actually exists and has an historical right to use that registered name.

Whether it is a fine, ordinary or poor wine is another question. Only your tastebuds know for sure.

Q. What do the letters V.D.Q.S. mean on a wine label?

A. If you find them on anything but a French wine label your suspicions should be aroused to start with.

V.D.Q.S.

Vins Delimites de Qualite Superieure (wines of superior quality from delimited areas) is the second of three general quality classifications for French wines. The first being A.O.C. and the third V.C.C. Fully 80% of French wines fall into the third level or below, or may not even be worthy of any rating.

V.D.Q.S. wines represent about 10% of French production - close to 200,000,000 gallons annually. The French government controls the areas, the variety of grapes used in their production, and the yield per acre for this category. So, in effect you do have a French government blessing upon such wines. Of course, they'd bless French milk if they could export it at those prices, too.

But this classification is of some value and there is often a bargain to be found among the more than 50 wines that can be marketed under this banner. During good years some of these V.D.Q.S. wines will overlap and surpass the lower end of the A.O.C. or Appellation Controlee wines.

Some of the more popular names you may come across, bearing the V.D.Q.S. title, are Coté de Provence, Costieres du Gard, Corbieres, Minervois and Cotes du Luberon. Within each of these groups, quality will also vary considerably as many different merchants market under these titles. So don't let one sample satisfy your curiosity about them, as if it ever could. Experiment, Experiment, Experiment!

Q. I've been told that France, aside from making many of the best wines in the world also makes some of the worst. Is this true?

A. The bottom of the barrel is no stranger to French wines.

The Good, the Bad, and the Shifty

On either the northern coast of France near Dunkirk or on the southern near Sete, one can find a curious little grouping of huge underground tanks, a main pumphouse and a nearby laboratory. Upon first sight you might think it's an oil depot set up for refueling ships.

A sea-going tanker slips into dock, is pumped full, and quietly it sets out for destinations unknown. It's filled to the gunwales with cheap wine, not expensive Arabian oil. Companies such as these can mix any wine your imagination can create. A few hundred thousand gallons of a nice Rosé, you say - why not? Just pump 50% of a bitter Corsican red wine and 50% of a dull Spanish white - blend - and voila . . . the perfect Portuguese Rosé.

French wine merchants of this calibre buy cheap wines not only from France, but from anywhere - price is the chief factor. Algeria, Puglia (in Italy), Sicily, Corsica, Spain, Morocco, are noted suppliers. The Common Market allows that if blended in France, such wine can still bear **Produce of France** labels.

Even if you're not quite so ambitious, you can always get a tanker-truck full of a Liebfraumilch blended to order, or a Bordeaux from

Spain. If these charlatans were labelled for what they were and sold at appropriate prices, there would be little room for complaint. Yet, this is not the case; you'd be dumbstruck at the well-known labels that dress some of these wines.

But where are such disasters headed? Almost exclusively to countries with free enterprise distribution systems for wine . . . like the U.S. and Britain. The screen erected by Liquor Boards in Canada makes it impossible for such frauds to get through to the Canadian consumer.

Yet, despite all of the inferior wines that emanate from France, she still makes more fine and great wines than do all other wine countries put together. You just have to know which is the Good, the Bad, and the Shifty.

Q. What is CLARET wine?

A. The answer depends upon which country you come from.

Claret

In all other lands, aside from England, Claret has a very loose definition and can describe any light red table wine. In the United States you can label almost any red wine a 'Claret' - maybe even fermented tomato juice would pass. Some producers have bottled a Claret and a Burgundy from the same tank. So, it's hardly a term a wine drinker can put his trust in.

In France the expression has no acceptable meaning and has no legal recognition or status. In Canada, well . . . a 'claret' could be just about anything.

Now, that's what it isn't . . .

What it is . . . is the English name for red wines which came from in and around the French city of Bordeaux, on the south-west coast of France. Once upon a time, merry olde Englande ruled that part of France (for some 300 years) and Bordeaux was the capital city of their province of Gascony. It was certainly a great way to beat the import tariffs.

That explains why Claret is known as the "Englishman's wine."

Chapter XII

And also why so many famed Bordeaux Chateaux bear such Anglo-Saxon monograms as Chateau Talbot, Palmer, Barton, etc. Each and every red Bordeaux could be called a Claret, in these terms of reference.

So if you just happen to be popping by your local English wine merchant and see a few bottles labelled 'Claret' you would probably be safe in assuming they were red wines from the Bordeaux district of France. But that's all. It says little or nothing for quality. In fact, you can almost be assured it will be of lower quality or else it would be labelled a proper "Bordeaux."

If you see it in this country, about the only thing "Claret" assures you of, is that, odds are it will be red and not white.

Q. **Is it true that the St. Emilion wines of Bordeaux use different grapes than other red Bordeaux wines?**

A. Yes - but it's all in the family - the Cabernet family.

Cabernets

France's famed Bordeaux region has two outstanding sub-districts which produce much of the world's most superb red wine - the Medoc and St. Emilion. Both have their own distinct character and reputation. But, the Medoc seems to have the edge, in at least the volume of truly great wines produced.

The river Gironde on the southwestern coast of France, and its tributaries, geographically separates these two Bordeaux districts. But much more divides the two wines themselves. The grapes to start with. The predominant variety in the Medoc district is the renowned Cabernet Sauvignon while the Cabernet Franc is king in St. Emilion. Other grape varieties such as Merlot, Malbec, Petit Verdot etc., in small quantities, are frequently blended with the Cabernets to impart certain desired qualities to the finished product . . . like Merlot which is added for its fine bouquet.

Sauvignon is a smaller less productive grape than the Franc. Yet, it yields a longer-lived, slower maturing wine . . . this due to its higher tannin content. But both are truly outstanding wine grapes . . .

at the top of the grapepile.

Names like St. Julien, Margaux, Pauillac are world famou as Medoc villages. Chateau Lafite, Chateau Margaux, Chateau Latour, Pontet Canet are just a few of the Medoc wines known and loved the world over.

Some St. Emilion wines of repute are Chateau Ausone, Cheval Blanc, Chateau Figeac and Chateau Pavie.

Both cabernets are grown widely in South America while the Sauvignon is the chosen one in California. Both are strangers to Canadian vineyards.

Q. Would you explain what was so important about the year 1855, with reference to wines?

A. It was the vintage just after 1854 and right before 1856 . . . I think?

Classification of 1855

If I'm guessing correctly, what you're after is the classification of some famous French wines in 1855 and not that tired old line above.

Sadly to say I've heard this date of 1855 mentioned too often, as if it was indeed, the most important event in wine history. The tendency it seems, is to over-rate the significance of what took place that year.

In actual fact, it was the classification, of the French wines, or a noble attempt anyway, in the Medoc and Sauterne districts . . . nothing more. Of all the vineyard regions on our globe, and even all those in France alone, only the wines of these two Bordeaux districts were classified. It was conducted by a committee of wine experts as well as wine brokers in preparation for the "Exposition Universelle" to be held in Paris that same year.

In all, only 83 of the "creme de la creme" of the wines of these two districts were rated. Consequently, many deserving wines even in these regions were overlooked . . . not to mention the seemingly unforgivable act of totally ignoring all the wines of the St. Emilion region, many of which would have rated higher than some of those considered. It was more fashion and fad than good taste that kept other areas from being considered. However, in all fairness, we must admit those wines rated and put in certain classifications then, are still generally deserving of their rating today.

There are some of those 83 wines that today deserve to be upgraded and others who no longer live up to their rating in 1855. Yet, basically the classification is still valid despite some recent changes. Other parts of Bordeaux were classified in 1955 and Burgundy followed that first classification by ranking some of its wines in 1861.

Q. What are the wines of Graves like?

A. Typically French - if we had to answer in two words or less.

Graves

If you mentioned the word Graves it more often summons to mind the White wines from this famed Bordeaux district. But truly, the dry red table wines that emanate from here are not only more plentiful but enjoy a more distinguished reputation overall. Perhaps it's due to the fact that they rarely use "Graves" on their labels, that costumes their place of origin.

The word Graves itself means "gravelly soil". And it's more than simple coincidence, I can assure you, that that is precisely the nature of the soil in this district. Since there are other areas with a similar type of soil the Graves district is more properly called Graves de Bordeaux.

White Graves are most frequently labelled "Graves" or "Graves Superieure." Sauvignon Blanc and Semillon are the two prevalent grape varieties used. The wine is dry, straw-coloured and distinguished by a touch of moelleux (softness). For the most part the wines are **ordinary**, some being **fine**; with rare exception, none are really considered 'great' wines.

Graves red wines are rarely labelled such; usually coming to market with Chateau or brand names. Some of these stand with the great red table wines of the world - names like Chateau Haut-Brion,

Chateau Carbonnieux, Chateau Haut-Bailly, Domaine de Chevalier, etc.

The Cabernet grapes predominate for these red wines but usually produce wines softer, less distinguished than those from the Medoc. Their bouquet is also quite distinguished from the reds of other parts of Bordeaux.

Q. Why is Chateau Lafite considered to be the best wine in the world?

A. Because for red table wines, year after year it is just that . . the best wine this world produces.

Chateau Lafite-Rothschild

We don't want to create the impression, however, that each and every year Chateau Lafite is 'numero uno'. But it ranks first, close seconds and thirds with such regularity, that overall no other red table wine quite matches it.

In the Classification of 1855 in Bordeaux, Chateau Lafite was ranked first and in the more than 100 years since no other wine - albeit there are a few noble contenders - has taken the 'king of the grapevine' award quite so consistently.

But you may still wonder, why? From 150 to 200 acres comprise the annual vineyard plantings at Chateau Lafite. Only superior grape varieties like the Cabernet, Merlot and Petit Verdot are used and skillfully blended to lend the finished wine their individual superior qualities.

The Chateau's fermenting rooms are a model for this type of smaller winery . . . modern but, the grape is still allowed to do most of the work. It is not hurried or interrupted chemically. Peerless vintners here produce approximately 15,000 cases of wine each year . . . wine that has incomparable breed and class, a flavour that has more depth than most wells, a fragrance to shame most flowers and an aroma and bouquet matched by few wines in the world. That's Lafite.

The Chateau's renowned cellars hold precious samples of this wine that go back into the late 1700's. Chateau Lafite's 70, 80 and more than 100 years old have been drunk with remarkable pleasing power. They are not only just vinously alive but possess such astonishing quality if you ever tasted one you would never have had to ask why Chateau Lafite reigns supreme in the 'wonderful world of wine.'

Q. What identifies a true Burgundy wine?

A. Other than an exorbitant price tag, too much to consider in one small article.

Burgundy

The acreage of the Burgundy region of France, now under vine, is less than half of what it was in the late 1800's. And Burgundy wines are vinted from grapes that are famous for low yields per acre.

The average vintage from the complete district represents less than 1.5 percent of France's annual harvest. If you subtract all the ordinary wines from this total you are left with less than one third of one percent of the country's harvest classified as true Burgundy wines.

So, you don't have to be a financial wizard to realize what little Burgundy wine there is will always be high priced and on the way up.

The region of Burgundy, in the heart of France, consists of several very distinctly different districts, none of which claim to be Burgundy itself. All these sub-districts have outstanding and renowned reputations of their own and they seem quite content to be known by their own personal names.

Names such as Cotes de Nuits, Chablis, Cote d'Or, Chalonnaise, Maconnais and Beaujolais are among the who's who of the wine world and all are true Burgundies. Wines like Beaune, Montrachet, Meursault, Chambertin, Pouilly-Fuisse and many, many more have set the hearts of wine fanciers a flutter for generations. Not to mention lightening a few pocketbooks along the way too.

Burgundy - among the Royalty of wines - is becoming more expensive with each vintage.

Chapter XII

Not unlike temporal kings, Burgundy, this King of the 'wonderful world of wines', accomplishes both of these feats rather well.

Q. One of my favourite wines is Chablis. But I don't know much about it. Could you enlighten me a little?

A. Enlightening someone is rather a lofty goal . . . but I can tell you a little about Chablis.

Chablis
(pronounced - shab lee)

The name itself is recognized throughout the world as one of the most outstanding and finest of all white wines. Depending on vintage, it can be truly, a "great" wine. From the top down it comes labelled as Chablis Grand Cru, Chablis Premier Cru, Chablis and Petit Chablis. Your wallet and tastebuds will tell you the differences.

The little town of Chablis is located southeast of Paris at the northern most part of what is loosely called the Burgundy district. A genuine Chablis is very expensive today due to the high recognition factor of its name and a very limited almost static production level.

The quality of Chablis can vary to extremes from year to year, although the price not so much. When poor it is thin and much too tart. When great, it is a pale straw colour, has a clean, almost metallic taste and is bone dry. The grape used exclusively in its production is the famed Chardonnay.

Especially from the United States you will find a number of very poor imitations. Chablis outside of France could be as different as grapefruit juice and over-ripe mangoes. From those who imitate it, there is usually little respect for its heredity or its authenticity. Their only desire is to take financial advantage of the reputation Chablis has achieved.

The closest local substitute would be a Chardonnay or Pinot Chardonnay, named after the grape. They are now being produced in very limited quantities by some Canadian wineries. But caution is advisable: make sure you ask if it is 100% Chardonnay and has not been blended with any of our native varieties. That's like mixing apple juice and chocolate milk.

Q. A dinner guest recently brought a bottle of wine called Puligny-Montrachet made by Paul Bouchard. We didn't drink it that evening. Is it a good wine and should we keep it or drink it right away?

A. First, I'd like to know who the guest was. I want to invite him to dinner soon.

Puligny-Montrachet

Without question this is one of the finest, most famed, and expensive white wines in all the 'wonderful world of wine.' It retails at $9.00-$12.00 a bottle in Canadian liquor outlets. But not knowing the vintage of that particular bottle, I can't tell you 'to drink or not to drink.' About four to five years of age is best, though. Don't wait too much longer.

This Puligny Montrachet by Paul Bouchard et Cie. comes from the general district of Puligny Montrachet, not one of its specific vineyards. So it is most likely a blend of several different vineyards of the area and would not be considered one of the better examples of this famed district. Don't be too disappointed, though; it would be considered extraordinary in any other wine region.

The Burgundian district of Puligny Montrachet consists of 200 acres under vine (Chardonnay grape) and produces about 500,000 bottles each vintage. Some of the most celebrated offerings from this area would be **Montrachet** itself, the 1971 vintage selling for about $33.00 a bottle. **Chevalier-Montrachet** (1971) is also available for about $31.00 a crack.

Some noteworthy examples, but of slightly less renown would be **Puligny Montrachet Les Folatieres** selling for about $15.00 a jug and **Puligny Montrachet Les Combettes**, slightly less in price.

The wine itself is characterized by outstanding qualities. It's a pale gold in colour, dry but not offensively so, a touch of lusciousness in the taste, and it has a bouquet that'll knock your nose off. It's worth every cent you pay for it.

I still want to invite that guest to dinner.

Q. What is so unique about Beaujolais wine?

A. It's youth and price tag, to start with.

Beaujolais

Beaujolais is traditionally considered to be a Burgundy wine. But, in fact is quite different from traditional Burgundies. The Burgundy wines we know and cherish so much are derived almost exclusively from the Pinot family of grapes. While Beaujolais comes from the Gamay family . . . some authorities do contend there is a family relationship between the two, though.

Geographically, the Beaujolais district is at the southern end of the Burgundy region. It's clay and granite soil differs considerably from the limestone prevalent in the Cote d'Or.

Yet, despite its rather distant relationship to the famed Burgundian bloodlines, Beaujolais wines are truly among the most agreeable red wines in the world--fruity, full-bodied, with a special, almost spicy flavour that is absent of all harshness.

Indeed, it is famed for its youth. Rarely will even the best Beaujolais improve after three years of age. Ordinary Beaujolais is a light, eminently drinkable red wine, low in alcohol, about 9%-10%. Its life-span should be counted in months not years. Yet, its price is still respectably high.

Beaujolais Superieure is a slightly better grade, heavier in alcohol - 10%-12%. Beaujolais Villages is again one step up and must originate from thirty-five specified communes or villages, the name of the village often appearing on the label after the name Beaujolais.

One final plateau on the Beaujolais scale remains - yet you will rarely, if ever find the term Beaujolais on their labels. They originate from nine villages, are the best of Beaujolais, but are sold under their own village names. The nine are: Brouilly, Cote-de-Brouilly, Chiroubles, Fleurie, Chenas, Julienas, Moulin-a-vent, St. Amour and

Morgon. Because of not being as well known as the name Beaujolais, on rare occasions you could at one time find them for less money than some ordinary Beaujolais! Not cheap, just less. This has all but disappeared as more wine lovers have become aware of this.

Q. My favourite wine is Chambertin. Is it not one, if not THE best red wine in all the world?

A. It all depends. If you're from Burgundy, there's not a better wine in the world. But, if you're from Bordeaux, it's only **one** of the world's best.

Chambertin

In the heart of the Cote d'Or region of Burgundy lies a 69-acre vineyard, that to some degree, sets the world standard for red wine. Thirty-seven of these acres belong to the Clos de Beze but they too, are legally entitled to use the name Chambertin.

All together, they produce less than 75,000 bottles of exquisite wine annually. That's just one reason for their praetorian price tag. And they're not what you'd call newcomers to the scene, either. For, they've enjoyed considerable renown since 600 A.D. One of their more notable customers and avid fans was Napoleon himself.

These 69 acres are further divided among a number of different growers, the majority of which estate-bottled their own small vintages. But, surrounding Chambertin are a number of vineyards producing wines of somewhat less distinction.

They're grouped under the designation Gevrey-Chambertin. The poorer wines of this commune (still very fine wines, indeed) come to market as just that, Gevrey-Chambertin. Finer grades use the same term, only followed by a vineyard name. While, those closer to Chambertin geographically-speaking, as well as quality-wise, are entitled to a "Grand Cru" designation (Charmes-Chambertin for example).

If you're still interested, Chambertin sells in Canada at $20.00 to $30.00 for a 26 oz. bottle and there's no refund on the empty.

Chapter XII

Q. What does the term 'Blanc de Blancs' mean in reference to Champagne?

A. Literally 'Blanc de Blancs' means 'White from White'. In Champagne terms - a white Champagne from white grapes. Suppressing your urge to yawn and utter a passive . . . so? Read on.

Blanc de Blancs

In olden days of yore, about thirty or forty years back, expressions still retained a degree of stability for at least reasonable periods of time. They were not quite so quickly butchered and adulterated by usage of an indiscriminate nature. Blanc de Blancs, then, referred only to White Champagne made from white grapes. What makes this worth pursuing was that Champagne was and is traditionally vinted from a mixture of both white (green actually) and black (dark blue) grapes. The dark skins are removed before they can tint the juice red during fermentation.

Blancs de Blancs Champagne, those made only with white grapes, are more delicate, lighter, pale green-gold in colour, and more elegant in character. But they lack the body and ageing qualities of normal Champagne. For the most part they emanate from the French villages of Cramant, Avize and Le Mesnil.

Some nimble mind might rightly ask, if there's a blanc de blancs Champagne, is there such a thing as **blanc de black** Champagne? Yes! Small quantities of **blanc de noir** Champagne are made from the famed Pinot Noir grape. It is heavier and softer, but less distinguished than **Champagne** Champagne, made from the traditional mixture of both grapes.

More recently though, our term under discussion has loosened up even further and has come to mean any white wine made from any white grape (so goes tradition). Areas like the Loire Valley and the Provence district, to name only a couple, now produce Blanc de Blancs wine. What has made the term - in these and other districts - rather meaningless is that they never did make white wines from anything but white grapes. Black grapes were used only for red wines. But that's progress for you.

Temperature-controlled tanks can be used for cold storage as in the Champagne district of France (above) or for cold fermentation as Sebastiani Vineyards does in California (below).

Chapter XII

Q. Does Champagne only come from France?

A. Do Volkswagens come from Germany? Is Lasagne Italian?

Champagne

True Champagne originates in a delimited area of France - is vinted exclusively from certain varieties of grapes and is produced by a method that is tightly regulated. All of these factors are meticulously controlled by the French Government and the association of Champagne makers.

If you can match this little trick you can call your product Champagne. But until you buy a vineyard in the Champagne district of France, you only have an imitation.

Even if you matched the methods of production, ageing and used exactly the same varieties of grapes, it would never be the same product because the soil of that area of France imparts its own unique flavour and quality to the grapes. This is reflected in the end product and is part of what gives Champagne is inimitable character.

If you design, produce and market your own unique style of automobile, you deserve to retain sole use of the name you choose, if it is also unique. Have you ever seen a car sold as a Ford-like vehicle, or a Yugoslavian Chevrolet? Hardly! These companies wouldn't put up with even the vaguest infringement on their product rights.

Rarely are imitation champagnes made from the same grapes or are they aged as long. In France wines similar to champagne cannot be called Champagne and are termed, Vin Mousseux. In Germany, their version is called Sekt and in Italy, Asti Spumante.

But those lands who insist on selling a local product as Champagne not only poach on the reputation others have spent so much to build or to create, but rarely do they do credit to their own product. It too deserves its own unique distinction - or perhaps, it doesn't at that.

Q. What is a Chateauneuf-du-Pape?

A. Certainly not the Pope's summer house in France.

Workers bring in the Champagne harvest primarily by hand.

Chateauneuf-du-Pape

But it was, once upon a time. The fourteenth century Avignon Popes summered at the Chateauneuf (literally new castle). But the seat of the Papacy was soon to leave France and move to a little town somewhere to the east of Avignon - called Rome, I think. Anyway, the castle is now in ruin and Chateauneuf-du-Pape possesses a more secular reputation. Today, it is also the name of a village a dozen or so miles north of the French city of Avignon.

As a wine Chateauneuf-du-Pape is quite notable, a fine wine indeed, but its true stature is unfortunately preceded and overwhelmed by its recognition factor, which has grown steadily in the past decade or so. To the point where demand far outstripped production. The natural result - up went the price (what else). So for five years or so it was considerably overpriced - not at all a good value dollarwise.

New plantings in recent years have increased the volume of Chateauneuf-du-Pape available to the consumer but now the travesty - much is drunk far too young. As well, the quality has lowered somewhat as the price has receded slightly.

But now, to the wine itself . . . it's a sturdy wine, deep crimson in colour, full bodied and quite high in alcohol (usually around 14%). It's drinkable in three years or so but, best between five and ten years.

A dozen or more grape varieties blended together are responsible for its unique character. The most prominent varieties used to produce Chateauneuf-du-Pape are the Syrah, Grenache and Cinsault. They are grown on coarse gravelly soil upon which it seems impossible to grow anything, let alone fine grapes.

Despite its unjustified higher prices it is still a very fine wine. If a bottle does find its way into your collection, do yourself a favour, wait till it's at least five years old, or more, before you enjoy it - for enjoy it you will.

Chapter XIII

Italy

Q. What does the expression "Marchio Nazionale" mean on a wine label?

A. Since it's the mark of the Italian Government you're not likely to find it on the label of anything **but** Italian wines.

Italian Wine Terms

Marchio Nazionale (literally National Seal) is indicative of the Italian government's authorization for that wine to be exported. While itself necessary, it says little for the overall stature of the wine.

While we're examining Italian wine labels we might do well to consider a few other Roman wine expressions you're likely to run across.

Vendemmia for example, simply means the vintage or year of harvest. It's invariably followed by a year designation.

There are also three denominations indicating something of the origin and nature of the wine in each bottle 1) **Semplice** (unblended) 2) **Controllata** (controlled) and 3) **Controllata e garantita** (tested and guaranteed). These expressions will usually be preceded by the words **Denominazione D'Origine.** So you're likely to come across such an expression as **Denominazione D'Origine Controllata,** etc.

According to the Italian Wine Law of 1963 **Semplice** indicates of a specified district, made from the traditional grapes of that area in the traditional way. No inter-regional blending is allowed for these wines. It comes from where it says it does.

Controllata is more controlled as to grape breed, yields per acre, vinification methods, ageing and bottling procedures. Such wines must meet these standards.

Controllata e garantita indicates wines of special note and that they have undergone numerous tests and tastings to establish their quality. As well, the producers of such wines must file documents with the government proving their claims.

Q. Is Est Est Est a good Italian white wine?

A. It is! It is! It is!

Est Est Est

Just in case anyone missed that clever rsponse, probably because your Latin is as rusty as mine . . . "EST" is latin for "it is." Anyway . . .

Even better than the wine itself is the story surrounding its name. Although it's an oft repeated tale I might as well add my name to the long list of tale-spinners.

It seems one wine-loving German bishop was on his travels to Rome, around the early 1100's. Apparently not wishing to sojourn too far without a cooling, restorative sip of the grape he dispatched a servant a day or so travel ahead . . . to pre-taste the fare available at inns along the way. The servant was instructed to chalk mark on the wall of every tavern that served wines especially good, the word "EST" . . . thereby indicating to the following bishop the better places to stop for the odd tipple.

But alas, when our faithful servant reached a small hilltop town some 60 miles north of Rome, Montefiascone by name, he was so impressed by the wine of one tavern he enthusiastically chalked EST! EST! EST! on the door of the inn.

The good bishop simply couldn't pass up such a promising pleasure and stop at this inn he did. He tasted and tippled, tasted and tippled some more, until finally he toppled himself into his grave (still to

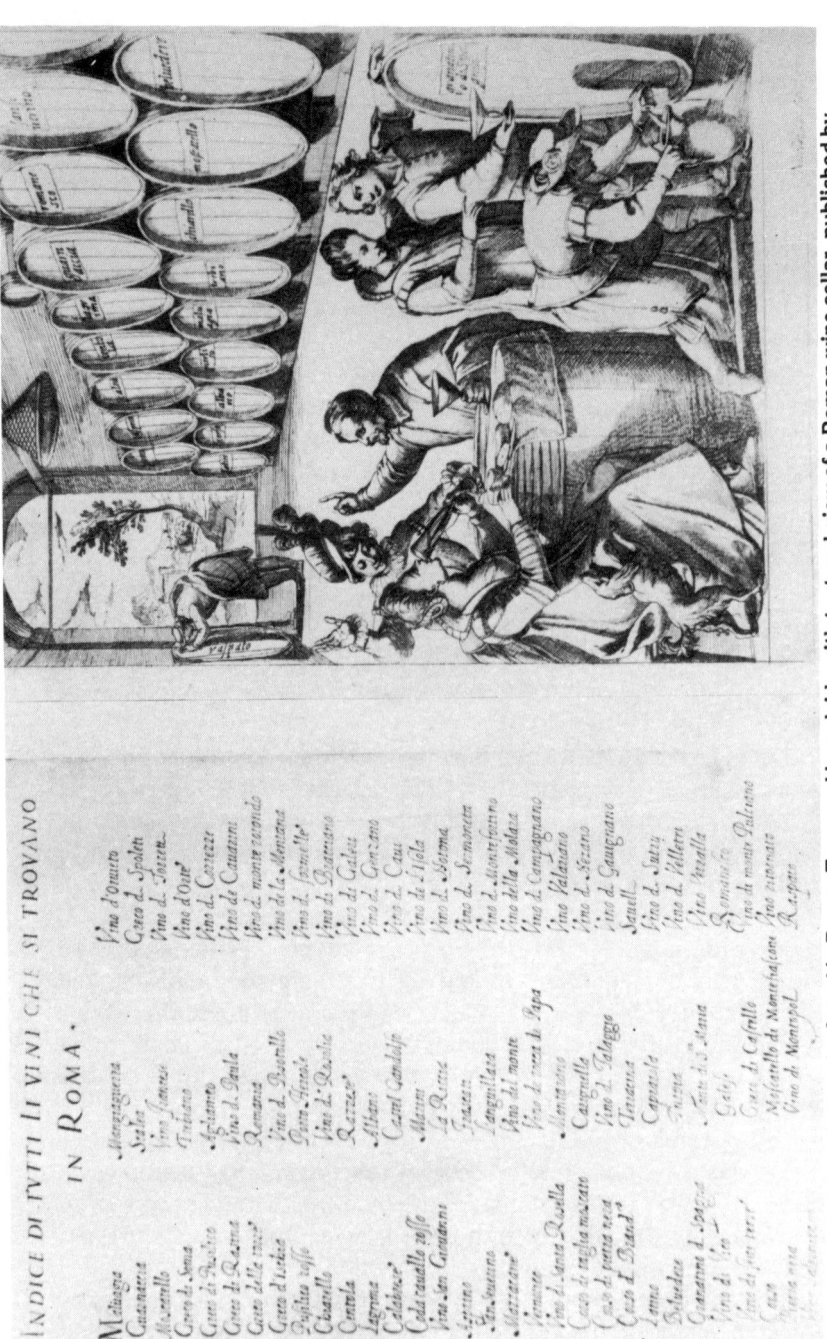

List of all the wines to be found in Rome. Engraved broadside with text and view of a Roman wine cellar, published by Nicolaes van Aelst, Rome, early 17th century.

Chapter XIII

be seen in the town).

Whether or not it was a long dusty road between inns or the sheer delight of the wine that caused the poor bishop to drink to his demise, it may never be known. But one thing is for sure . . . EST EST EST is not likely to induce any modern replay of this event.

Today EST EST EST is available in a light dry version as well as a sweeter offering. Neither are outstanding . . . noble indeed, but hardly worth losing your head over.

Q. What is the difference between the two Italian wines Bardolino and Valpolicella?

A. Dirt . . . believe it or not!

Bardolino e Valpolicella

Both are red wines from the province of Verona, Italy. Both come from the area around Lake Garda. Both are vinted from the same grapes - primarily the Corvina, Negrara, Molinara and Rondinella. Yet, despite all these similarities in heredity and environment, the two wines remain quite distinct.

The reason is unquestionably the soil. Valpolicella vines are grown some ten miles to the east of Bardolino on a somewhat heavier clay soil. The resultant differences are easily detected by a trained palate.

Bardolino is a very light red wine, hardly deeper in colour than some Rosés. It is light in alcohol as well, 9 to 11-1/2 percent by volume. Though it could never be considered **great** it is a charming wine, bright, fruity, clean and fresh. And there's little doubt it should be consumed by the time it is three years of age. As a carafe wine for summer refreshment, it is ideal. If it doesn't bear a vintage date - ask why and then buy another brand of Bardolino.

On the other 'mano', its brother Valpolicella has slightly more grace and breed. It is fuller than Bardolino, higher in alcohol (11 to 12%) and can be held to its fifth birthday before drinking.

It has been described by some connoisseurs as fragrant and velvety. In my opinion, both adjectives are well deserved. Valpolicella

Superiore is bottled only after eighteen months in wood, which indeed contributes to its loftier stature.

All the aforementioned only goes to show you . . . you can come from the same family, grow up in the same neighbourhood . . . yet still be in a class all your own.

Q. Where does Marsala wine come from?

A. From Sicily via Liverpool

Marsala

Around the middle of the eighteenth century some Liverpool merchants were looking for a wine they could produce that would fit in with the current English vogue and appetite for sweet wines, like Sherry and Port. At last they discovered a place on the island of Sicily near the town of Marsala. In the surrounding vineyards grapes similar in nature to those used to produce Port, Sherry and Madeira were found.

A couple of notable English families were quick to set up shop and not too many years passed before the Marsala wines were being shipped back home; Lord Nelson being one of the more famed customers. Since that time Marsala wines have forever had their ups and downs in courting public favour.

Like Sherry, Port and Madeira, Marsala is a fortified wine (alcohol added to bring it up to 15-20% by volume) and is truly one of the world's unique and fine dessert wines.

The wine is fermented until it is bone dry. And then a grape syrup which has been boiled down till it is thick and caramel-like in colour, is added along with grape brandy. The end product of this careful blending is then aged in cask for a number of years before bottling. Dry Marsalas are also available and are blended similarly to a Spanish solera.

A fascinating and delicious dessert can be made very simply with a sweet Marsala wine.

Chapter XIII

Zabaglione

Beat well together 1 cup of sugar and 6 egg yolks. Add 10 ounces of sweet Marsala wine. Cook this mixture in a bain-marie, or in a double boiler, over a low heat, whisking it vigorously until it becomes frothy and stiff. Cool. Serve in wine glasses, alone or with fresh well-drained fruit cocktail . . . or - cool quickly by putting the top pan in cold water without ceasing to whisk. Quickly add 1 cup of stiffly whipped cream. Mix and serve as above.

Q. What should you look for when you buy a Chianti wine?

A. Since there's chianti, Chianti and CHIANTI, you should know what you're after - a pizza partner or an elegant accompaniment for a filet.

Chianti

Basically, there are three types of Chianti. And we are talking only about those from Italy, not the imitations trumped up in other parts of the world and labelled something like a Chianti.

What separates 'chianti, Chianti, and CHIANTI'? Essentially the quality and the time they are ready to be consumed. Certain Chiantis are made to be drunk young, very young. The only glass container they're ever likely to see is the wine glass into which they are poured. These Chiantis come straight from the vat to the table. But none of this type is available in Canada.

The second type of Chianti is also meant to be consumed during its youth, but it actually reaches the bottle for a short time. The straw-covered **fiaschi** which contains most of this variety of Chianti has probably done more to popularize Italian wines than all other devices. Yet, from this same type of Chianti comes most of the international disappointments and complaints. And it's becoming ridiculously overpriced in Canada.

Because this is the major type of Chianti exported. It reaches maturity so quickly often by the time the overseas consumer gets it, the wine has already reached its peak or has begun to decline somewhat. Some mistakenly hold on to these wines thinking age may improve a little. So when you purchase Chiantis in the straw-covered flasks, the younger the better. They are not a wine that will be enhanced by age.

The third example of Chianti, also exported to Canada, is Classico Chianti. These wines are among the royalty of the Tuscany district of Italy, where all true Chiantis originate. Not only do these wines age well, but they are among the most long-lived table wines in the 'wonderful world of wine.' They are indeed fine wines, some vintages even great and though more expensive, are worth every penny. You will find them in plain glass Bordeaux style bottles sans the wicker cradle.

Q. What's the difference between a Chianti and a Classico Chianti?

A. About $2.00 a bottle . . . and something called quality.

Classico Chianti

All true Chianti originates in the Italian district of Tuscany. All 50-60 million gallons of its annual offering (4 times as much as all Canada produces each year). Chianti wines are produced from a blend of several different grapes; primarily the Sangiovese, Black Canaiolo, Malvasia and Trebbiano.

As mentioned in an earlier article, there are three basic types of Chianti. The first two are wines to be enjoyed in their youth. These wines are also made by a unique method of production, called the "governo" method.

From 3 to 10% of the grapes are held back and dried or raisined. After the fermentation is completed for the other 90%, these raisined grapes are crushed and added to the already fermented main batch. This causes a second fermentation in cask and gives a slight prickly, fresh taste to the finished product. These Chiantis are fruity, youthful wines and are intended to be drunk in this very condition. Age, is for the most part, their enemy.

Classico Chianti is quite different. It comes from a specifically defined area within the major Chianti region and is vinted by the standard, single fermentation method, not the "governo" process. And it appears in the market place not in the traditional straw **fiaschi** but in a Bordeaux-style bottle.

With Classico varieties, the word **Chianti** may or may not appear on the label, and then perhaps only in a secondary position. Some Classico names to look for are: Brolio Riserva, Riserva Ducale, Villa Antinori and Nipozzano - all fine wines of outstanding ageing ability. Some of these can be laid away for ten to thirty years and confidently served when opened.

You may not be able to hold your breath that long, but don't worry, Classicos can be enjoyed by the time they become available at your local outlet. For in all probability they will have already spent five years in cask and perhaps even added years in bottle. They are well worth the extra $2.00.

Q. What part of Italy produces the best red table wines?

A. If you're Italian and your name is Bruno - whatever area you come from.

Piedmont

But, for the rest of us non-Romans, the northern part of Italy, especially the district of Piedmont produces the majority of Italian wine of world renown and reputation.

The district of Piedmont squeezes out one hundred million gallons of wine a year, give or take a million gallons or so. This district is on the same latitude as the southern part of France and its Rhone and Provence districts. Oftentimes a comparison is drawn between the wines of both these districts - which doesn't make either the French or Italian vintners too happy.

Perhaps, the finest of the wines from this district is Barolo, a slow-maturing, big red wine. It spends three years in cask and once bottled stands the test of time for years to come.

Some experts feel the only Italian wine to give Barolo any serious competition would be a Gattinara, which is made from the same Nebbiolo grape. It seems that a number of Italians feel the same way, because it's very hard to get a Gattinara outside of Italy. Although it doesn't bear its age as well as Barolo it possesses a little more finesse and finish. But that just means you don't have to wait so long before you can drink it - if you're in Italy that is.

But, if you can't wait till you get to Italy try another fine offspring from Piedmont, a Barbera. Barbera is somewhat lighter than either Barolo or Gattinara but it has a price you can't refuse.

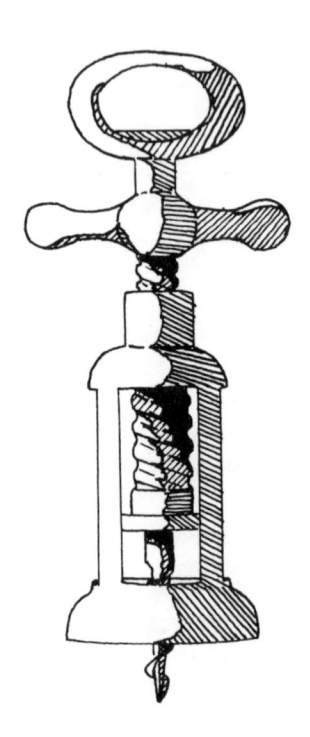

Chapter XIV

Germany

Q. A friend told me that true German wines are made only from the Riesling grape. Is this true?

A. Your friend may have told you that . . . but you'd better inform him not to tell any German winemaker that story!

Not Riesling Alone

Muller-Thurgau, Sylvaner, Bodensee, Breisgau, Ortenau, Markgraflerland, Kaiserstuhl, Gewurtztraminer, Gutedel, Rulander, Spatburgunder, Elbling, Kerner, Portugieser, Trollinger, Scheurebe, Morio-Muscat . . . are but some of the different grape varieties grown in Germany today. And all make 'true' German wine.

In fact, as important as the Riesling is to the international fame of German white table wines it is not the quantity **king** of German vineyards. Actually, it places third, to Sylvaner's second. Undisputed first place, as far as quantity is concerned, is held by the Muller-Thurgau grape (a cross between the Sylvaner and Riesling).

The 1975 harvest showed results of approximately 35% Muller-Thurgau, 27% Sylvaner and 25% Riesling. Yet, when we're talking about quality not quantity, in German white wines, we are talking about your friend's favourite.

In this instance Riesling is definitely the unchallenged **King** of

German vineyards. One simply has to consider the regions in which the Riesling grape predominates ... the Rheingau, about 80% Riesling and the Moselle about 70%. These two regions alone originate more famous German wines than do all others combined.

The true Riesling grape (Johannisberg Riesling) grown outside of Germany, and to be fair Alsace as well, produces wines of a very different nature. So really there is no substitute for German white table wines made from this grape. As well, there are a number of imitations made from so-called Riesling grapes such as the Gray Riesling, Emerald Riesling and so on, whose resemblance to a true Riesling is more in the imagination than actual fact.

Q. What makes Moselle wines different from other German wines?

A. Primarily geography but the colour of the bottle is different too.

Moselle-Saar-Ruwer

The Moselle River starts in France, as do many other good things, winds its way through Luxembourg and eventually ends up in Germany where it joins the Rhine River near the city of Coblenz.

Wines that are produced along the banks of the French part and the section running through Luxembourg are all of quite ordinary quality. The more northerly the river gets, the better the wine produced, the best coming from latitudes about the same as Winnipeg.

There are some 20,000 acres under vine in the Moselle region alone, producing more than 10 million gallons of wine (almost as much as the total Canadian vintage). The Riesling grape reigns supreme in the Moselle. And except for 6,000 acres or so of outstanding wine production the rest yields wines similar to most typical German Rieslings, a little thinner, more delicate perhaps.

The soil, a peculiar kind of slate, seems to be the factor which produces outstanding white wines on that unique 6,000 acres. In great years it imparts to these wines a delicacy, a bouquet that puts them in the running for the most distinguished white wine in the world award.

Low in alcohol, pale, spicy, flowery, they have a distinctive breed which clearly separates them from even the great Rieslings of the Rhine. Truly a joy to experience.

And they come in green glass bottles instead of the brown from the Rhine. Most provincial Liquor Boards list a Moselle . . . so, try one soon (you vill like it).

Q. I was stationed near Baden-Baden in Germany while in the service and enjoyed the local wines. How do they compare to other German wines?

A. Baden-Baden wines are gooden-gooden.

Baden

Actually, Baden-Baden is just one of many towns in the German province of Baden, which just coincidentally is also a specified wine region, one of 11 in Germany.

The vineyards of this region are numerous and extremely diverse in nature but primarily they are planted along the foothills of the black forest and overlook the Rhine River as it flows northward. Since there are such variations in the topography and the variety of grapes planted, the wines of Baden are numerous and quite different from each other.

There is nearly 12,000 acres under vine in this region and it produces 78% white wines and 22% red. The predominant grape variety is the Muller-Thurgau (a hybrid cross between Riesling and Sylvaner grapes) accounting for a full one third of the overall harvest. The famed Riesling grape itself only represented 7% of the 1975 yield.

This will no doubt explain why we can describe, in general terms, Baden wines as agreeable, 'noble', some even 'fine' wines, with a very rare few if any, that could ever be considered great. But alas, very few Baden wines are ever exported. So don't get your tastebuds worked up to sampling Baden wines. This is just an exercise for information sake.

However, should you decide to visit Germany and in particular the Baden region make a point of stopping at the Kaiserstuhl. This is an extraordinary spot. It looks like a miniature mountain rising out of the fertile Rhine Valley - festooned with terraced vineyards. Some very notable wines originate from this spot. In this case you have to go to the mountain to taste these gooden-gooden wines from Baden-Baden.

Q. I've heard so many different explanations of what Liebfraumilch is! Which is right?

A. I don't know which ones you've heard but here's another one.

Liebfraumilch

Until 1971, when German Wine Laws changed drastically, Liebfraumilch was a rather dubious, catch-all term used in the broadest fashion, to denote certain Rhine wines. Usually, the wines were poorer, low quality examples of German viticulture.

However, the name (meaning "milk of the blessed mother") became so well known some better quality wines started using the name as well, in an attempt to cash in on its popularity. The result - a very broad, undependable quality range of wines sported the **Liebfraumilch** label.

But that's all changed!

Starting with the vintage of 1971 Liebfraumilch must meet very stringent criteria. It is now designed a **Qualitaetswein** and must meet all standards for this designation, such as: registration at picking time (to insure the origin of the grapes) - only wines from four districts, Rheinhessen, Nahe, Palatinate and Rheingau can use the name - government analysis at bottling time - blind tastings by experts - it can only be made from Riesling, Sylvaner or Muller-Thurgau grapes - it also must reach a minimum sugar content.

So with 700 years of history behind it Liebfraumilch is finally a name you can put some trust in - that is for being what it's supposed to be - a fine regional German white wine . . . nothing more.

With all this upgrading in quality and dependability you don't need anyone to tell you what happened to the price of Liebfraumilch - up by about 25%.

Q. One of the best German wines, Schloss Johannisberg, used to have different coloured Caps to denote certain qualities. What has happened to them as a result of the new German wine regulations?

A. Nothing! They're alive, well, and living in the Rheingau.

Schloss Johannisberg

Perhaps, in advance of answering your question directly, some background information on Schloss Johannisberg might be in order. To say Schloss Johannisberg stands atop the world of white wines, is almost an understatement, that's how grand is its reputation.

Physically, the vineyards of the Schloss are only about 85 acres in size and produce a mere 600,000 litres of wine annually. But, their elegance, bouquet and fruitiness have made them worthy of the highest praise. The vineyards are located on a low hill overlooking the Rhine near the city of Mainz in Germany.

Since the late 1700's the Riesling has been the exclusive grape used in this vineyard. However, vines and wine from this piece of real estate go back to the eleventh century. Sample bottles from each of the consecutive vintages are in stock, starting from the year 1842 onward. And there are yet, two bottles of the 1748 vintage in the Schloss' wine museum.

Until 1971 the wines of Schloss Johannisberg were sold with red, green, pink, white, orange, blue and gold tops or capsules; each representing a different quality or type.

Today, all such colours fall under the new 1971 German wine law as "Qualitatswein Mit Pradikat," and are now classified as follows:

Red and Orange	· Kabinett
Green and white	· Spatlese
Pink and blue	· Auslese
Gold	· Beerenauslese & trockenbeerenauslese

Q. A client of mine introduced me to "Icewine." Can you tell me something about it?

A. Firstly, what it isn't, is wine with ice cubes in it!

Eiswein

And I wouldn't advise anyone to start encouraging a taste for it - unless you have more than your share of patience and money. Icewine or **Eiswein** comes from Germany, where it is a rather sporadic phenomenon. A number of unique circumstances must prevail before Eiswein can be produced at all.

When grapes are left late on the vine, to mature and gain added sugar content, occasionally a frost will occur. When temperatures unexpectedly drop in late November or early December to perhaps 20 deg. Fahrenheit, following a dry fall season, some of these grapes still on the vine will be caught and they will freeze. Grapes with lower sugar content would be frozen solid, but these with their high sugar content are only partially frozen.

They are then picked early in the morning and crushed before they thaw completely. The resulting "must" or grape juice is very sweet, thick, - almost a syrup. The wine vinted from this juice resembles the sweet German "Ausleses."

But patience - remember? 1842 was the year of the first recorded production of Ice Wine. And in the over 100 years since there has only been 10 or so years when the conditions were just right to make this unique offering.

1961 and 1972 were the most recent years when Icewine was produced. Expensive? Absolutely! And you'll have to **special** order them from your local outlet. You're looking at $25.00 a bottle and up . . . and up . . . and up . . .

Chapter XV

Some Other Vinelands

Q. What are the best Rosé wines?

A. It's difficult to single out one rosé from the bouquet of rosés that are offered on the market today. Some are quite different and purposefully so. Some so different you might mistake them for a watered-down cream-soda.

Rosés

Rosé wines are experiencing a singularly notable upswing in popularity in North America, but seemingly for all the wrong reasons. This is not to say there is something wrong with drinking rosés, but all too often they are the compromise when you don't know whether to serve a red or white wine. Truly, they deserve better treatment.

There are considerable variations in types of rosés. The most significant rosés come from France. The Loire Valley of France (Anjou) produces rosés of a sweeter, luscious quality. They are available in still and crackling varieties.

In France's southern Rhone region is found the most highly regarded Rosé, Tavel. It is drier than the Loires, is noted for its prominent bouquet and higher alcohol content. Your particular tastebuds will decide which is better for you even though connoisseurs generally agree Tavel is at the pinnacle of the Rosé bush.

Other lands such as Portugal are making their presence known in the world of Rosés. If honestly made they are pleasant, palatable wines, growing in stature and public acceptance, perhaps more because of massive advertising campaigns rather than individual merit. Nevertheless many foods go well with them and they are especially enjoyable when served well chilled.

Q. Recently I have been drinking a Hungarian wine that I find quite good and excellently priced. It's called Szekszardi. Could you comment on it?

A. More than comment on it, I enjoy drinking it, too.

Szekszardi Voros

And you are right, it is an excellent dollar value where everyday wines are concerned. Indeed it's been responsible, to a large degree, in forcing Canadian wineries to take a second look at their efforts at producing an affordable **vin ordinaire.**

Szekszardi Voros means "a red wine from the district of Szekszard." This district is found in the largest wine growing region in Hungary, the Great Plain, called Alfold. It lies between the rivers Danube and Tisza.

Szekszardi Voros is vinted from the Kadarka grape, of which little is known - as far as its heritage is concerned. In fact it is almost impossible to compare it to any other grape in Europe. Some efforts, years ago, were made to relate it to the mysterious Zinfandel grape grown in California. Yet, the wines bear little resemblance in character and the theory has been pretty much abandoned by most experts.

The colour of Szekszardi Voros is almost a pomegranate and it has a spicy aroma peculiar to this region. Despite its deep colouring it's not a heavy red wine and averages about 12.7 percent alcohol by volume.

Its character is that of an 'ordinary' wine but it has enough depth to be considered a good **vin ordinaire.** After tasting both 1969, 1971 and 1975 vintages there appears to be little difference. It would indicate that considerable regional blending is taking place. If it was officially classified by its land of origin as a **fine** wine it would more than likely be labelled **Szekszardi Kadarka** instead of Szekszardi Voros. But for the price . . . who's complaining?

Q. An American friend told me they make wine in his home state of Ohio. Do you know anything about Ohio wines?

A. Not much, practically speaking . . . for its glory has long since faded.

Wines of Ohio

Before the civil war tore apart that nation, Ohio was the most significant wine producing region in the United States. The Finger Lakes region of New York state and those sunny California vineyards were mere upstarts in comparison.

The vines of Ohio were planted along the Ohio River to the east and west of Cincinnati. Apparently the steep hills that overlook the Ohio River reminded some German settlers of their beloved Rhine. They just couldn't resist planting a few vines. The vines prospered and by the mid 1800's wines from Ohio were demanding as high a price in New York City as most imported wines. The dominant grape variety in this region was the infamous hybrid Catawba . . . both still and sparkling versions were popular.

Several decades later more vineyards sprang up along the south shore of Lake Erie west of Cleveland, a few even on Lake Erie islands. A promising future seemed to await Ohio wines . . . in fact it was booming right on into the early 1900's.

Prohibition brought all that promise to an abrupt halt, though. The vines were ploughed under, by law, and Ohio wines have never fully recovered.

Today, there are still several million gallons of Ohio wines coming to market each vintage, consisting primarily of native North American varieties and a number of European hybrids. As yet no Ohio offerings are available to Canadian consumers through our Liquor Boards.

Early American vineyard scenes. Vines along the Ohio (above.) The Vintage in California (below). Hand-coloured wood engraving from Harper's Weekly, 1878.

Chapter XV

Essentially, those once famous vineyard slopes along the Ohio River are still waiting for a generous application of that infamous old 'Yankee ingenuity' from some enterprising wine lover . . . to rekindle the Ohio wine spirit.

Q. I've noticed some wines from Chile appearing on our Liquor Board shelves lately. Are they any good?

A. According to the Chilean Ambassador - they're excellent.

Chile

And if we counted 'time in the business' they should fulfill their Ambassador's fondest expectations. For Chile's wine history goes back into the early 1600's.

Surprisingly Chile ranks 9th in the world production of wines and 6th in per capita consumption. Again, it is the famed European species of grapes that predominate Chilean vineyards.

Most of their vineyards are situated in Chile's fertile central valley not far from Santiago. Although their grapes are European and they follow traditional French viticulture methods, the wines are markedly different to their European counterparts.

This is due primarily to a vastly different climate and largely a volcanic-type soil. Their wines have a perceptible 'earthy taste' (gout de terroir) especially their reds. But as with many other smaller wine producing nations little of their finer wines are released for import. Importers of Chilean wine seem to concentrate their efforts on lower priced wines. Subsequently, it is difficult to get an accurate picture of their viticulture expertise.

Their varietal labels (Rieslings, Pinot Noir, etc.) are more dependable than their brand names and some day if their political situation stabilizes we may well be seeing more of their finer wines, usually designated as **Reservado** or **Gran Vino**.

On a quality scale of 0-100 current Chilean imports to Canada would average in the low sixties. Not bad but with all due respect to their Ambassador - certainly not excellent.

Q. Australian friends visiting recently highly praised their native wines. How good are they, really?

A. As good as anything else that grows upside down!

Australian Wines

My first task though, in discussing Australian wines must be to forever dispell an ill-founded rumour. Australian grapes are absolutely **not** 'pressed out' by herds of marauding kangaroos . . . despite the fact that their pedal extremities appear ideally suited for the task.

With that behind us we must also set aside any impression of kangaroos merrily bouncing through fields of wild grapes away back into Australian antiquity. For, like the white man, grapes are immigrants, transplants to Australian shores. But, both now seem to be doing quite well, thank you.

The first grapevines were planted in Australia around Sydney in 1788. Eventually some 600 varieties of European vines found their way into Australian vineyards.

Grapes flourish in all but one of the Australian states today but South Australia, New South Wales and Victoria account for most of the annual vintage. The **vendange** or grape harvest starts in January and is usally over by late March.

Australia produces about 5 times as much wine as we do in Canada but use strictly the tried and tested European varieties . . . thusly on the whole, they produce superior wines. Although, Canada's gradual switch to European varieties and hybrids in the past few years has narrowed the gap considerably.

Although small quantities of very fine wines are produced in Australia, blending and a number of other factors combine to cut short Australia's attempts at producing significant quantities of truly **fine** wines.

Q. My heritage is Austrian. What do you think of Austrian wines?

A. If my heritage was Austrian I'd probably say 'they're the best.' But since It's not I'd have to qualify them as pleasant, passable wines.

Austria

Traditionally, Austria is a wine-drinking country. The inhabitants consume about nine times as much wine as we Canadians do, on a per capita basis. They import a great deal more wine than they produce, which fact tells us why we see so few Austrian wine labels on our shelves. Austria is one of Italy's very best customers.

The better wines of Austria are almost invariably white. They're fruity, relatively dry, have a good 'nose' but are characteristically low in alcohol. They resemble the German whites of Baden as well as the Italian whites of Tyrol. They are definitely not for laying down in your wine cellar; drink them while they're young.

Many Austrian wines sport varietal (grape names) labels such as Riesling, Sylvaner, Gewurztraminer and local notables such as Veltliner. They will, on occasion, be designated **Spatlese** and **Auslese**. But unlike their German counterparts they are not as sweet.

The Austrian offering Canadians are most likely to see at local outlets is a Gumpoldskirchener, from the famed town of Gumpoldskirchen. (Where else?) The name is often followed by a varietal grape name and may be designated Spatlese or Auslese. They are fresh, light, pale, fruity and are good values. They can be **fine** wines indeed, but they never aspire to genuine **greatness.**

Austrian reds aren't really worth mentioning, so I won't.

Q. Could you tell me a little about the wines of Greece and particularly a wine called Retsina?

A. It seems, as went the Greek nation, so went their wines.

Greece

Greece was once a respected world power, a leader in culture, art and philosophy. Her wines were no less significant. The modern role of Greece, however, has diminished considerably and so have her wines.

However, as a volume producer of wine Greece is notable, producing about 10 times the volume of Canadian production. And coincidentally, the average Greek drinks about 10 times as much wine as the average Canadian.

Greece makes a good deal of sweet fortified wine such as Samos from the Muscat grape and Mavrodaphne from the grape of the same name. Some are of fairly good quality but there are no outstanding wines.

A good deal of Greek table wine is flavoured with resin or retsina. This practice essentially eliminates these wines from any international favour. The resin imparts a **turpentine** flavour to the wine and only those who have cultivated a taste for it, appreciate its presence.

The pine tree resin is added to the grape juice during fermentation at a ratio of about 1 to 99 parts of juice. Several stories speculate the reason for its addition. Some say the resin was believed to be an antiseptic during any epidemics (for internal application only). Others claim that young wines were at one time aged in fir casks and people got used to the taste this wood imparted to the wine. At length they started adding resin to duplicate the taste.

Accept whatever rumor you prefer, but unless you've got a little Greek in your background you're not likely to become a fan without considerable effort.

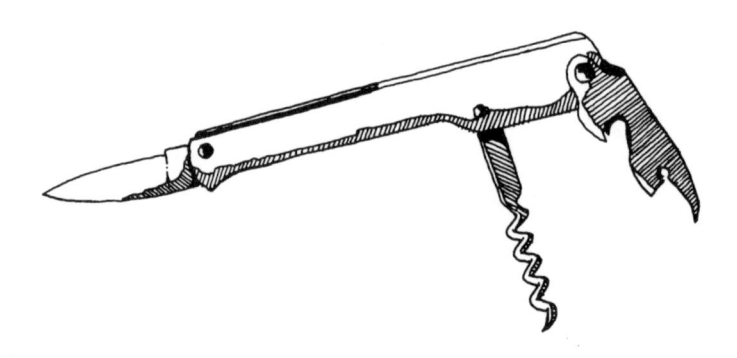

Chapter XVI

Wines With a Kick

Q. Is Vermouth a true wine?

A. Despite its keeping regular company with the infamous Gin gang, it hasn't yet been disowned from the wine family.

Vermouth

The name Vermouth originates from the German word WERMUT, meaning wormword. What does wormwood have to do with Vermouth, you ask? Basically, Vermouth is a flavoured, sometimes even a fortified wine. Human handling and expertise have more to do with the end product than they do with table wine, for example. It's a contrived wine.

A number of 'aromatics' are used to give Vermouth its unique aroma and flavour. The chief aromatic ingredient used is the flower of the Artemisia Absinthium · better known as 'wormwood'. Other aromatics used, include bitter orange peel, camomile, cardomon, aloes and occasionaly anise.

Straight up or on the rocks, Vermouth is a very popular aperitif. But, one of its more famed usages is its minor role in the renowned Martini.

There are two significant types of Vermouth · Italian and French. Traditionally, Italian Vermouth is darker in colour, sweeter and heavier in both body and taste. It comes primarily from Turin province in Italy and is usually made from the Muscat grape.

The French product is usually quite pale in colour and very dry. Occasionally these lighter coloured Vermouths are slightly higher in alcohol content, so sometimes a bit more expensive.

And just to keep you on your toes, France does make the darker Italian type of Vermouth, too. And Italy also makes the lighter French style, as well. Then again, a number of other countries make both. Decisions, decisions, decisions . . . But, despite using similar ingredients the originals seem to stand apart from the newcomers.

Some trade names to look for are Martini & Rossi and Cinzano with Italian characteristics and Noilly Prat and Cazapra with the French flair.

Q. Is it true you can keep Madeira wine for 50 years or more?

A. Maybe you can - but I can't. My tastebuds can't wait that long?

Madeira

But it is true. Madeira wines can be kept for a century or more and be enjoyed to the full when opened. Of course, it would have had to be one of your ancestors who started it all off . . . for you to enjoy a 100-year-old Madeira.

Winston Churchill, awed by tasting a 1792 vintage Madeira, exclaimed: "Do you realize that Marie Antoinette was still alive when this wine was made?"

The word Madeira itself covers a number of different wines originating from the Portuguese island of Madeira. Four main varieties of Madeira, all named after the grape used to vint them, are best known outside the island.

There is **Sercial,** a dry **aperitif-type** Madeira, contrasted most sharply by **Malmsey** (from the Malvasia grape) an excellent, sweet dessert wine. In between are **Verdelho**, not quite so dry as Sercial, and a **Boal** or **Bual**, though not as rich as Malmsey is fuller and more fragrant. All are genuine Madeiras.

Chapter XVI

Madeira wines are made by a unique process and owe their ageability to this method of vinification. After a rather normal fermentation period and a dosing of grape brandy, the young wine is placed in an **estufa** (hothouse) where it is gradually heated to 114 deg. F. and held at that temperature for 3 to 6 months.

After another 4 years, at least, in cask or vat, there appears a wine possessing singularly unique properties. One its longevity, another being its affinity with the kitchen. Truly, no other wine can compare with it in this regard. Any French chef worth his salt will openly admit this.

And oh yes, aside from ageing it and cooking with Madeira, you can drink it - right now. You really don't have to wait 50 or 100 years.

Q. What makes certain wines like Port and Sherry so sweet?

A. It all depends on which kind of "sweet" you mean: sweet as in "sugar-sweet" or sweet as in "how sweet it is" - an expression often heard from those in the port and sherry business to describe their booming annual sales figures.

" . . . Sweeter than wine"

Assuming that it's sugar-sweet you meant, we can say that, the originals, both Sherry and Port, owe their sweetness to natural grape sugars and not to the addition of cane sugar, this being the case so prevalent with many imitations.

Port from Portugal is made from grapes famed for their high sugar content. At some medium point in the fermentation process a grape brandy is added which halts the fermentation before all of the natural grape sugars are converted into alcohol. The result, a wine with a sweeter character, varying according to when the vintner added the brandy.

Sherries, as they're produced in Spain, are allowed to complete their natural fermentation process and become very dry wines. After the ageing process the wine is doctored or **dosed** with a **super-sweet** grape-wine that has been concentrated by a boiling process.

Sherries range from very dry, **Fino**, to very sweet, **Oloroso** or

Cream, with infinite gradings in between. There's one to suit any taste.

Many different countries produce Sherry and Ports, some making even more than Spain and Portugal. But rarely do they have as much to offer. So, if you want a treat, stick to the originals . . . "how sweet it is!"

Q. What is the difference between the four different types of Sherry?

A. The difference is, that there are five main types of Sherry, not four.

Jerez - Xeres - Sherry

Jerez (pronounced Haireth) is one of a number of sunny, festive but unknown little Andulucian towns in the southwestern corner of Spain. But, with the name Sherry, it's known and appreciated on a world-wide scale. It's been the venerable home of Sherry wine for well over 2,000 years.

Twenty-thousand acres of vineyards (about the same size as all Canadian vineyards combined) make up the authorized zone for Sherry production. The Sherries we know and treasure so intimately fall into five very basic classifications: **Manzanilla, Fino, Amontillado, Oloroso** and **Cream**.

MANZANILLA: the lightest of all Sherries. Very pale, light to the taste, very dry. As the vineyards face the Atlantic, the bouquet of the wine has almost a salty tang. An excellent accompaniment for shell fish.

FINO: very pale in colour. Very crisp and dry taste. Has an aroma of fresh flowers and fruit. As with Manzanilla, it should be served well chilled. Ideal with most seafoods.

AMONTILLADO: amber-coloured. Pungent, hazel-nut aroma. Mild and full, it is medium-dry. Best served with cheese, soups or salads. The perfect compromise between those who prefer only dry or sweet Sherries.

OLOROSO: the colour of burnt gold. Soft and mellow bouquet.

Slightly sweeter than Amontillado, with a touch of walnuts in the taste. Suggested as an appetizer or a dessert wine at the end of the meal.

CREAM: rich and luscious-tasting. Darker, reddish-brown in colour. Preferred by most North Americans because of its added smoothness and sweetness. Can be served as a liqueur, at room temperature or slightly lower.

Q. What is a 'Solera' Sherry?

A. Better yet, what is a Sherry without a Solera?

Solera - Sherry

True Sherry and the **Solera** are inseparable. The only place that you're likely to find a Sherry that doesn't call a Solera, home, are the cheap Sherries being made in various countries other than Spain, the originator of Sherry.

More recently, however, some lands outside of Spain have started to develop their own Soleras and thusly you'll come upon certain domestic Sherries labelled **Solera Sherry**; as if there were ever anything else. But what is a Solera, you still ask?

A Solera is a system by which a wine, like Sherry, is aged and matured while being progressively blended. The purpose - to produce an end product that is consistent year after year - a product with characteristics the same now as they were ten years ago. Of course, this voids there ever being a vintage year for most Sherry. For each blend may have from half a dozen to as many as one hundred different vintages blended together.

The mechanics of the blending go something like this: if you can imagine a several tier or stage collection of barrels. In the top row of barrels are the youngest wines. These are left to age for a while and then are blended with the next group of barrels down. Each new vintage goes on top and gradually makes its way, after many blendings to the bottom row. This is of course, a simplification of what actually takes place.

From this bottom row, so to speak, comes the wine that is

finally bottled and reaches you. A skillful cellar-master who knows his job, can produce an outstandingly similar Sherry, year after year.

So, despite the imitations, true Spanish Sherries all come from a Solera, but you'll not usually find that word on their labels.

Q. **What is Flor Sherry?**

A. Certainly not the bottom of the barrel!

Flor Sherry

In many wine growing regions around the world a certain yeast (unicellular microorganism) of a particular strain will dominate and may be totally unique to that one area. They play a large role in establishing the final character of that particular wine. The same grapes vinted with different strains of yeast would produce wines of identifiably different attributes.

Flor (Spanish for flower) is such a yeast. It is native solely to parts of the Sherry region of Spain and to Chateau Chalon in France. These microorganisms are airborne and collect on the grape-skin. When grapes are pressed to make Sherry and these flor yeasts start to work, some other rather strange events take place later on.

Soon after the fermentation when the Sherry casks are not quite full and the wine is exposed to the air in the gap, a film starts to form on the surface. It multiples until it forms a layer (resembling a cottage cheese), as much as an inch thick, . . . a **flower** as the Spanish say.

This film of Flor yeast imparts to the wine a very distinctive flavour and a bouquet and oddly, prospers only on the drier, lighter wines. In Spain, the results are Fino and Amontillado Sherries.

California, Australia, South Africa and Canada are now successfully producing wines resembling Sherry that also have the unique Flor yeast qualities. Of course, they must import the Flor yeast itself. However, even with the imported yeast, for years they all experienced difficulties in achieving dependable results, often not being able to induce the **flor** reaction at all.

Chapter XVI

A supposedly Canadian development (an agitation method) overcame the problem resulting in an improved product from all of these countries. Yet, despite notable results, they continue to be just that . . . notable imitations.

Q. How can you make your own Cognac at home?

A. The best way is - don't. Your Cognac may be ageing in oaken barrels while you're ageing in the local lock-up.

Cognac & Brandy

Cognac and **Brandy** are both distilled spirits (distilled from wine) and are quite illegal for home manufacturing. Even if you had the facilities the fruitage of your labours would bear little resemblance to the originals. And besides, who wants to spend the rest of their life dodging the **revenuers** as many a Kentuckian might put it.

Cognac, Brandy from the Cognac district, is officially defined this way: "It is the result of the distillation of the white wines produced inside the strictly delimited Cognac area (France), distilled with the old fashioned Charente-pot still, in accordance with local habits and aged in oak wood casks."

To distill a home-made Cognac that in any way resembles a true Cognac, is like asking for the best way to make your own Rolls Royce. It's sheer folly to even try.

Brandy, on the other hand, is not quite so demanding. It's produced by distilling almost any white wine and is made and known by the name Brandy in many different countries including our own. But not so with Cognac.

The Cognac district itself is divided into several distinct areas and from these originate a variety of quality levels. One has to be cautious when buying Cognac as there are some shippers who make good use of certain myths surrounding Cognac. This enables them to sell their wares at higher prices. So there is no substitute for a brand name and a shipper who has preserved a consistently high reputation for generations.

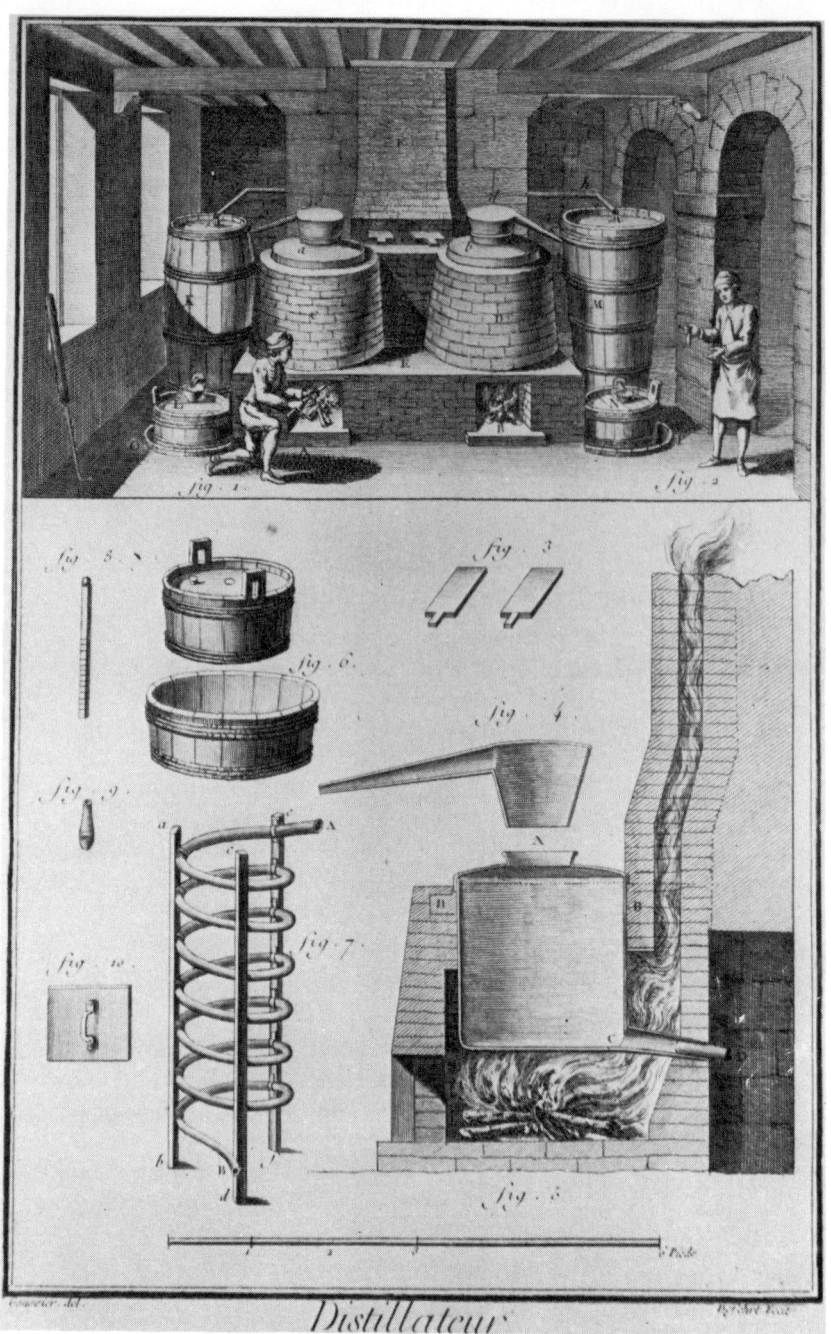

Brandy Distiller. Hand-coloured line engraving, Defehrt, Paris, 1762.

164

Chapter XVI

Q. What do the terms V.S., V.S.O.P., Napoleon and Champagne have to do with Cognac and Brandy?

A. Too often, their merit lies more in their decorative qualities on certain labels.

Cognac Terms

One of the more reliable symbols found on many a bottle of Cognac is the price sticker. One thing is certain, no Cognac producer is going to sell a high quality Cognac for the price of lower quality Cognacs.

However, though this is frequently the case, the reverse is not always true. Some lower quality Cognacs do sport price tags for far more than they're worth. They frequently get away with it by employing artistic packaging and liberal use of the above expressions.

Reliable historic evidence indicates that Napoleon, the first one, wasn't much of a Cognac or Brandy fan at all. He certainly didn't have any special casks of the best Cognac or Brandy cellared aside for his private use. So the term was and continues to be essentially meaningless. Some producers use this term loosely in conjunction with some of their superior products - but don't look for any guarantees that this is always the case.

Contrary to general thinking, the terms **V.S.** and **V.S.O.P.** really give no legal guarantee as to age. Originally these terms are merely ciphers used by many shippers as a matter of convenience, but their definition could vary with each shipper. They stood for; **Very Superior** and **Very Superior Old Pale.** Usage today is primarily out of tradition and often with little merit in themselves. They are a vague indicator of quality and age.

Champagne Cognac has nothing to do with the Champagne of **bubbly** fame. In the Cognac area there exists several districts, two of which are named Grande Champagne and Petite Champagne. These two districts generally produce the finest Cognacs and are genuinely labelled as such. A blend of the offspring from both of these districts often comes to market as **Fine Champagne** or **Grande Fine Champagne** Cognac. The three share at least one common quality - they are very expensive.

The Saint Emilion grape variety used to produce Cognac makes less than palatable table wine. Very shortly after fermentation, the wine is pot-distilled into Cognac.

Chapter XVI

Q. Which is better Cognac or Armagnac?

A. This is a question for which there seems to be no correct answer - at least not a safe one. Lovers of either are bound to take exception no matter how diplomatically you phrase your views.

Cognac vs Armagnac

Since we have commented on **Cognac** in earlier articles it seems only fair, and safe, to consider some of the merits of **Armagnac**, for a few lines at least.

Armagnac is certainly not as well known as Cognac but purports to have a history 200 years senior to Cognac. As is Cognac, Armagnac is a distinct district (defined legally in 1909) in France, but some 50 miles to the south of the famed Bordeaux region (Cognac being situated just to the north of Bordeaux).

Armagnac's history is inexorably linked with D'Artagnan, the Three Musketeers and the famous cuisine of Gascony. The swashbuckling travels and exploits of the Musketeers may well have been responsible for the early spread of Armagnac's reputation in the mid 1600's. For it was supposed to be their favourite indulgence, since the Musketeers originated from the region of Gascony as well.

In our 20th century, Armagnac is produced in the age-old fashion from the Picpoul, the Jurancon, the Muscat and Baco 22-A grape varieties - whereas Cognac comes primarily from the Saint Emilion variety.

The unique soil of the Armagnac district and its different distillation (continuous distillation) methods also account for the considerable variances in end products, when compared to Cognac.

To speak in vagaries (much safer) Cognac is lighter than Armagnac, in both body and colour. While Cognac has its own distinctive bouquet, when warmed in a **pipette** Armagnac originates a fragrance and bouquet that is not only unique but unparalleled.

Both Cognac and Armagnac are high quality brandies. Which is best? Not me! That's one limb I'm not about to climb out on.

The famous "Le Peu" distillery used to produce Hennessey Cognac. The pot-stills are only in production a short time each year.

SECTION III

Distribution

- Controlled Distribution or Free Enterprise?
- The Dollars and Cents of It

Chapter XVII

Controlled Distribution or Free Enterprise?

Liquor Boards are a tight-lipped lot. Trying to squeeze in-depth information from them, concerning their **modis operandi** is like trying to get juice out of a raisin.
By in large their response to efforts in connection with researching material for this book was . . . well, I won't say hostile but words like curt, cool and cautious will give you some idea. And it's not so much that they didn't like you asking questions. They'd listen to your questions all day long . . . it's the answers I'm still waiting for. And it's not so much that they refused to give you the answers either . . . it's just the run-a-round you get. And it's not so much that I mind the odd run-a-round . . . it's just the length of the trip I object to . . . the track runs from Victoria to St. John's.
My greatest measure of success, however, came with the the Liquor Board of Ontario (LCBO) - perhaps only because I was closer and economics allowed me to be more persistent. At any rate they were my most significant source. But much of this information applies to all Liquor Boards. Necessity forces them to operate in a similar manner. So if we all can set aside our provincial prejudices for a short time we can get on with a look at how wines pass through the digestive tract of government distribution channels, while we compare the **control** system to **free enterprise.**

Chapter XVII

Two World Distribution Systems

Two very different systems of distributing alcohol-based beverages stand in growing contrast today. Government control, as in all Canadian provinces and some other countries like Finland, Sweden and Czechoslovakia for example - and the private enterprise system, as seen in 32 of the United States, in Britain, and many other lands. And long and hot has been the controversy over which is the more desirable . . . which better serves consumer interests.

On a continent that has traditionally fostered and thrived on free enterprise, the very existence of a government **controlled** retail outlet, a monopoly, for any commodity, runs against the social grain to begin with. And as one so public example of such a **control** institution, Liquor Boards are the targets of an incessant barrage of complaints, accusations, and charges of their being just another bungling bureaucracy. The Boards have numerous opponents - vociferous and determined. But are they correct? Is their badgering justified?

Some complaints, some accusations, and some charges of Boards being bungling bureaucracies were justly earned and once were well applied. But today, it's no longer a clear-cut case.

Indeed, both systems, private enterprise distribution and government control, have their individual strengths and weaknesses. But, by in large, the **control** systems comes out the winner in all but a very few comparative circumstances. That's if the criteria is benefit to you, the consumer. This personal view, of course, will be vehemently contested by any number of producers, agents and consumers.

A number of public and media personalities, who claim to be in the **know** on this subject, periodically take journalistic potshots at the Boards - with little fear of a rebuttal. After all, publicly favouring a government monopoly of any sort is hardly in vogue. Few, even from government ranks, are willing to climb out on this public limb. So, the impact of this uncontested sniping has, over the years, tended to create a negative disposition towards the **control** system - an attitude it no longer deserves much of the time.

So then, what makes purchasing a bottle of your favourite

indulgence from a Liquor Board any better or worse than buying it from Joe's Liquor Store? In the final analysis you are to be both judge and jury, but there are a number of factors for you to consider before rendering a personal decision. Because, at length you will decide which system prevails.

Despite periodic public whining by those who would instantly turn the sale of all alcoholic beverages over to private enterprise, Liquor Boards maintain a tenacious and monopolistic grip upon this function. And to this date, there is no credible move afoot to alter this arrangement. So, whether you're a fan or not, the Boards appear to have become established social fixtures, for the foreseeable future, at least.

The chasm that exists between these two distribution systems is best defined in four, broad basic areas. **Marketing - product selection - quality control - price.** And the real worth of each system is best established by a frank comparison with the other.

Marketing

One area of major advantage for the **control** system revolves around the very **marketing** or **selling** system itself. Not always, but more and more frequently today, the consumer falls prey to some rather wily devices employed by private enterprise.

From the moment you walk into any reasonably-sized private retail liquor store in Britain or the U.S.A., for example, you realize you are in a very different atmosphere, when compared to a government shop here in Canada. The first impression is visual. More often, attractive, tasteful surroundings are evident · brand displays are plentiful · special deals are conspicuously up front · **sale** signs are placed strategically to catch your attention. And not infrequently you will be approached by an eager member of the sales staff whose prime objective is to sell you booze. And the more the better.

This is in sharp contrast to the traditionally austere, virtually sterile settings chosen by our Liquor Boards, in past decades. And as far as being approached by a member of the staff, unsolicited · well, that would be a memorable event. You are free to browse at your leisure without harassment, if indeed, there is anything to

Chapter XVII

browse in aside from a listing board. And you know how exciting they can be.

However, recent efforts by the boards have been somewhat more artistic in nature. They have taken positive steps towards creating more welcomed and attractive surroundings. Self-service outlets are moving even further to overcome the impression that you are on a methadone program and you've just come in for your next dose. Charges that such progress has been too tardy are essentially true. But what movement there is seems to be in a pleasing direction. The Rare Wines and Spirits outlet in Toronto epitomizes what one truly would expect of a rare wine and spirit shop, tucked away on some cobblestone street in a quaint little English village. For a moment, several perhaps, you'll forget the government has any interest in the establishment. Filling out an order form quickly brings you back to reality, though. Well . . . you can't expect perfection.

In a private enterprise store either in the U.S. or England asking for assistance in selecting an appropriate wine, can be and too often is, asking for trouble. When you solicit such advice, the consumer, for his own protection, should be aware of the various motives behind the suggestions he'll receive.

Sales staff in privately owned stores, are prone to push various brands for economic reasons. Overstocked on one brand - you can be assured that will be the suggested wine until the situation is remedied. A few brands of wine over the hill a little - guess what? That firm may even have a special **arrangement** with a particular supplier, wholesaler or importer - you know those wines will be highlighted. Or, at best, you may simply be subject to an individual's personal tastes. Any staff member may have strong preferences or prejudices - they'll invariably be reflected in their advice.

The opposite is the case at Board outlets, almost to the extreme. In larger stores the Board may have a wine consultant on staff. But, for these consultants to specifiy one brand superior to another, could put their very job on the line. In contrast, asking in a smaller outlet, as I do occasionally just to see what response I'll get, well . . . that can be a one act comedy in itself. At this level some Liquor Board employees are so uninformed about wine I'd guess some would define wine as weak whisky.

Standing amidst a few hundred bottles of wine, no matter how orderly they're arranged, is a confusing situation for all but the most seasoned wine lover. When you ask your friendly Liquor Board consultant for assistance in choosing a bottle, you quite naturally expect a very positive response. Yet, the suggestions forthcoming may be so cryptic in nature, your plight could be worse than to begin with. In all fairness though, occasionally the field will be narrowed down by this rather neutral counsel, at least limiting your confusion to reasonable proportions.

Product Selection

Eliminating from both systems the larger outlets, with broad selections, you find the average store, the type you're likely to find in the corner plaza, has significantly less offerings from which the consumer can choose. And generally speaking, comparisons of these smaller, local outlets reveal Liquor Boards to be significantly ahead of private enterprise, where liquor and wine selection are concerned. Again, in general terms, private enterprise tends to stock far more low priced **specials** at this local level, than does your neighbourhood Board outlet. This seems to be its sole advantage, other than perhaps, offering home delivery.

Inducements, graft, pressures, and threats have riddled free enterprise distribution channels for alcohol ever since booze became a commercial commodity. It's no secret that organized crime takes more than a passing interest in alcohol products and their distribution. They cut their teeth on it during prohibition. From essentially innocent **inducements** to blatant bribery · from mild suggestions to corporal pressure · all have, and continue to play, an expanding role in some private distribution channels.

With respect for those reputable private merchants and agents, who maintain a degree of integrity, we must qualify these assertions as not applying universally. Yet, at the same time the intention isn't to soften the impact of what is increasingly the case today, even for some once highly respected private wine merchants . . .they cheat.

There are literally tens of thousands of brands of alcohol-based beverages. What is it that determines which labels end up on the

Chapter XVII

shelves of a private outlet? National and local brand preference, of course. They have to be there. But, that only accounts for a small percentage of the number of labels that might be available in any privately owned store; especially is this true for wine.

Buyers for such stores, chains of stores or wholesalers come under concerted pressure to stock certain brands or labels. Inducements and outright bribery in the form of money, product, and gifts can often be the governing factors for what you as a customer of private enterprise, first of all, are able to find on the shelf. Then add to this the various inducements which may cause the sales staff to tout certain brands and you may just begin to appreciate the freedom a **controlled** system can represent.

A large respected agency, representing European wine producers was known for his respectable volume of business on both East and West coasts of the United States. When asked why they had no customers in the central portion of the country, they hesitatingly admitted: "We were told to stay out." A short explanation . . . but, it says volumes.

Board Selections

Not only is consumer preference virtually the sole factor which determines a brand remaining on most Boards' shelves, but little (except shelf position in a self-serve store) can be done on the part of the Board to influence you at the time of purchase.

So, what is it then that determines the selection of brands you do find at government outlets? Firstly, no single individual decides what labels become listed or delisted. Today, a standard procedure remains almost the only road to getting a new brand listed with virtually all provincial Liquor Boards.

An agent first submits an official "Request for Listing" form. Aside from a complete product description he must supply such information as firm price and anticipated annual sales as well.

From this point samples of his wares are submitted to a series of rigid chemical analyses to make sure the product meets all the requirements set down by the Federal Food and Drug Act as well as the Liquor Control Act of that Province.

If the laboratory passes the wine, it's then submitted to a grading panel of tasters who further evaluate the stature of the product. The grading panel for the L.C.B.O. consists of six senior wine consultants, having a minimum of ten years tasting experience with the Board. Other Board wine consultants, juniors, also take part in the tasting but their evaluations do not count in the final judgment.

Each wine is evaluated in blind tasting, by a 100 point grading system. To be judged acceptable or, considered commercially saleable, a wine must rate on the average, higher than 60 points. How close do individual evaluations run? Without exception each of the six tasters will be within 1-3 points of each other. A **rookie** taster may be as much as 20 to 30 points off. The juniors, perhaps 7 or 8 points on occasion. But remember only the scores of the **six** count in the end. Senior consultants may taste as few as 20 to as many as 100 wines each week. The average wine rates about 65 points on this scale.

Having passed this rigorous requirement the wine is then in line for possible invitation into the Board's repertoire. Twice each year the L.C.B.O. sits to select new listings from those who have passed the inquisition. Not all who pass are assigned L.C.B.O. numbers and put out for sale. The Board isn't about to list, say 50 brands of Beaujolais, regardless of their all passing basic requirements. Supposedly only the very best are favoured, after balancing quality and price to the consumer. Brands that have been listed in past years are not set aside when a better one comes along, unless of course, sales of this brand drop below set quantities.

Orders may then be placed with the producers, selected stores receive stocks, but you, the consumer make the final decision as to whether the brand stays or at length is rejected. And you have two years to make up your mind. For, a certain volume of sales (it varies for each product type) must be attained over the trial period of two years. If not, it may be delisted. Remaining stocks would then be disposed of at the expense of the producer. The Board rarely, if ever, loses on a deal.

The consumer benefits invariably from these strict business standards, being also assured, for the most part, that the product line he has to choose from is there for the right reasons. Not because **inducements** or **pressures** were exerted on the people responsible for such product selection.

Chapter XVII

Despite persistent trade rumours that there are certain labels which have bypassed the standard Liquor Board listing procedures, illicitly finding a spot on the shelf, little in the way of tangible evidence exists that would prove such rumours. The possibility is always a reality, of course. And I dare say it would be a fair guess that Liquor Board defences have been breached by some influential peddlar on more than one occasion.

But due to the very complexity of the selection system and the necessity for each brand to achieve and maintain specified sales levels, just to hold onto that listing, our supposed offender, if not able to establish and maintain public acceptance, would eventually be spit out of the system like a tattered computer punch card.

Fraud Target

Outright frauds in the Liquor or Spirit trade are comparatively rare. Oh, there's always the odd jug of moonshine floating around. And watered-down bar-rye is infamous. But, on the whole, the liquor industry, in producing nations, is tightly controlled at the source.

However, recently wine has come under increasing consumer suspicion. The scandals in Bordeaux and the Chianti fiascos have made the public more sensitive and aware of what they are buying or think they are buying when it comes to wine.

With little fear of contradiction it can be flatly stated, the chief, if not the exclusive target of questionable wine producers are the private enterprise systems. Even when so-called reputable shippers have a disaster to dump, their target - private enterprise distribution channels.

The Liquor Boards employ such a seemingly energetic screen to counter these frauds, that few if any of these shoddy producers bother trying to penetrate it at all. After all, why try to crack Gibralter when private enterprise systems are so open and vulnerable. Not only vulnerable, but more often they prove cooperative and eager to grab their share of the ill-gotten gains.

So, while other parts of the world fall victim to wine frauds, in Canadian provinces, due largely to the control system, they remain essentially untouched by such scandals.

Quality Control

This opens for us the whole subject of quality control. In a free enterprise system the burden for quality control falls essentially on the shoulders of the original producer. There are a great number of trustworthy and dedicated winemakers, indeed, but there are many who aren't. And even more, who are not above the odd flim-flam when the right set of circumstances arise. Basically, the consumer is ill-equipped to determine which is the good, the bad, and the shifty.

Most localities where private enterprise outlets operate have local or Federal Food and Drug regulations with sections that apply specifically to alcoholic beverages. But monitoring is the usual weakness . . . sporadic and thin at best. And many of our shifty producers know enough to meet most basic food and drug regulations. Often their only sin is presenting a product devoid of most of the qualities which would commonly identify them as respectable wines. The crime - these common wines are often hidden behind a label or name that is widely known and respected. A name in which the consumer has considerable confidence as a quality brand.

Compounding this problem is the ebb of complete integrity within the ranks of private retail wine merchants and wholesalers themselves. Far too many are open to **bargains**. Some out of malicious intent, others simply can't distinguish between the good, the bad and the shifty, either. And if you've ever watched a sea-going tanker being pumped full of wine in an Italian or French port, you begin to realize where these **bargains** come from and just how much of a bargain they truly represent.

If such wines were sold for what they really are and priced accordingly, there would be, perhaps, little room for complaint. But if you were to follow that tanker till its cargo ended up bottled on someone's shelf, you'd be dumbstruck at the noble claims such labels often infer. True, some reputable wine merchants, retail and wholesale, have experienced consultants to analyze and taste products before they are put up for sale, but rarely is this sufficient to insure that consistent quality levels are maintained.

This is not to suggest all wine found in private outlets is of a fraudulent nature. Far from it. The majority is not. You just have to have your wits about you to be able to determine which is which,

Chapter XVII

the good, the bad, and the **bargain.**

A private merchant on the prowl for a deal has little trouble finding accommodation. For example, a quick trip to Dunkirk, on the northern coast of France or Sete on the southern, finds a company whose assets consist of a laboratory of sorts, a vast number of huge interconnected storage tanks, and a main pump house which can blend for you any type of wine your fancy may invent. And they can deliver by the truckload, the rail-tanker full, or even a sea-going tanker, filled to the gunwales.

The wine may come from Algeria, Corsica, Spain, Morocco, Sicily . . . anywhere they can get it cheap. But because it is blended in France, and the Common Market authorizes it, many of these **blends** will legally sport 'Produce of France" labels.

A Rosé you want . . . why not? Just pump fifty percent of a bitter Corsican red and a fifty percent of a dull Spanish white, blend, and guess what . . . a French Rosé . . . by the tanker full. In fact more wine labelled **Anjou Rosé** emanates from Puglia in Italy than from the Anjou district of France itself.

Where are those catastrophes heading? Britain, the United States, and any other **free enterprise** distribution systems with a taste for a quick buck. And that doesn't exclude many.

On a visit to England I stopped into a very reputable wine merchant's shop to pick up a bottle of red wine. It was to accompany me to a dinner invitation. To my delight, I found a bottle of Margaux (one of the most famous regions in Bordeaux, France). The price tag at that time was a more than reasonable £1.25 (less than $3.00). My better judgment questioned the price, but my curiosity eventually held sway.

Later, when the cork was pulled it soon became evident that the only time this wine had seen France was while the Spanish tanker passed the French coast on its way to Liverpool. What upset me most, was not being taken, even though I was supposed to know better, but **who** took me - one of the most reputable wine merchants in all the world.

This is not a unique or even an uncommon experience, though. A recent independent investigation by some of the world's most renowned wine tasters revealed that the average English shopper was better off buying his everyday, inexpensive wines in the supermarket. It was established that the traditional wine merchants were far more likely to **corkscrew** the consumer than their local grocer. Despite poorer selections from which to choose, the supermarkets displayed an enviable regard for integrity and fidelity, rarely found among the wine merchants inspected.

A good example cited was a villainous bottle of red wine labelled, St. Emilion 1970 **Appellation Controlee**. By all rights this should, indeed, have been a fine regional French Bordeaux wine. It was purchased by our experts from one of England's best known wine merchants. Upon close examination it was assessed, beyond any doubt, as being a Spanish wine, and a poor Spanish wine at that. When a further bottle was sent to **CIVB**, the Wine Growers Association of Bordeaux, for evaluation, their return comments were as follows: "A neuter wine without character which could not possibly claim the Bordeaux Appellation." This says even more than it appears to. For, some very ordinary wines have been legitimately labelled this very broad, Bordeaux Appellation Controlee.

At the risk of sounding repetitious, these events could not take place in Canada today . . . because of the Control system.

So then, just what are all these efforts expended by the Boards to insure consistent quality of product? As mentioned earlier, new products are subjected to demanding laboratory testing to determine that all government standards are met before the product can be considered for a listing. For Ontario's Board for example, frequency of inspection divides all alcohol products into three general classifications . . . Canadian liquor, wine and beer -- Imported liquor -- Imported beer and wine.

Canadian Wine

Canadian wine producers are quality checked on an annual basis. Each offering in their product line is scrutinized under these same stiff laboratory tests and must meet identical standards used for listing a new wine. Even wines that are not sold or listed through the Board (through independent wine stores) are checked annually. The Board has the authority to walk into any private retail wine store and randomly claim samples for laboratory testing.

Because of stringent internal quality standards followed by

Canadian manufacturers themselves, and constant monitoring by the Excise department to insure that it stays that way, yearly check-ups have proven satisfactory to guarantee that Canadian made products meet or surpass all basic quality requirements. And basic we mean. These quality standards lean more toward being of a clinical nature. They do little to establish the status of these products when compared to their world peers.

Imported Wine

Wine is a tempermental traveller. Especially table wine. Because of their lower alcohol content (9-14%) more potential problems exist during transportation. The fermentation process used to make wine is also fraught with more areas of weakness than is the distillation process of spirits. More can go awry, which may in the end ruin the wine. Added to this is, of course, its increased susceptibility to fraud.

For these and a number of other reasons every shipment of wine that crosses our border is subjected to laboratory analysis. If twenty shipments of a particular brand are received in a year, twenty separate series of checks are run on that product.

Interestingly, two sets of standards exist with the Board's laboratory - the Federal and Provincial regulations, and what is referred to by the Ontario Board as 'control' limits.

For example, the Federal Food and Drug Act stipulates wine shall have no more than 0.13 percent weight by volume of volatile or acetic acid (commonly called vinegar). But, if the wine industry, as a whole, is capable of limiting volatile acids to, say 0.01 per cent, then a 'control' limit is set at this point. So, a producer who submits a wine below the legal limit but higher than the 'control' limit is still warned about being too high and expected to remedy the situation. Although, not legally out of line, most producers take to heart the Board's suggestions - for their own economic welfare.

Truly, where quality controls are concerned there is little comparison to be made between the 'control' system and a private system, no matter how large or reputable. At best, the private retailer always carries with him a question mark concerning absolute integrity -- a question mark that is growing larger year by year.

'Control' systems despite their authentic shortcomings and all the potential dangers inherent in them as a monopoly, continue to offer a degree of security today's harried consumer rarely finds.

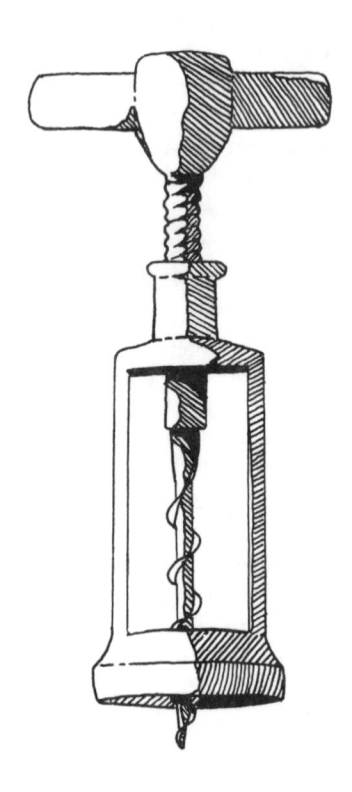

Chapter XVIII

The Dollars and Cents of It

Price can be the most versatile of all tools in the trade of retailing . . . and . . . never does a consumer scream longer or louder than when events touch his personal pocketbook.

Perhaps, these two economic and social dictums make it simpler for us to understand why the bulk of the charges journalistically levelled at the Liquor Boards revolve around prices.

First and foremost to come under fire, where dollars are concerned, is the profit margin added by the Boards -- as much as 112% in Ontario (for imported wines). Some provinces are less, some as low as 60% but this gap is slowly narrowing as their profits increase. Concerning this, there is no defense - and none is realistically offered by the Boards. They are too high. They're unwarranted and callous in today's marketplace. They should be lowered. Few Board officials will privately disagree.

But in their defense, the profit margin is not usually controlled by the Board. They are instructed to achieve certain profit levels by their Provincial Treasury Boards. And they must comply.

So, voices of complaint concerning profit margins, as legitimate as the complaints may be, if directed to the Board, are usually misdirected. You're talking to the wrong people. The Board does not have the authority to alter their profits. They are essentially a provincial government tool.

Associated with this exorbitant profit, is the frequent complaint that the profit margin is added after the Excise and Federal Sales Taxes (fixed by other Federal agencies, not the Board) have been imposed. In effect making an added profit, not just on the product, but on other agency taxes and duties that have been applied beforehand.

Of little consolation, rather more in the way of explanation, is the fact that this same practice is openly employed by private enterprise on imported goods of almost every nature. Perhaps, confusing the issue is that too many fail to distinguish the difference between separate government agencies, even between federal and provincial. Like private business, Liquor Boards, too, add profits after others apply their claims.

But, if some still feel it is reprehensible for one government agency to make added profit from another agency's taxes, then you must agree it's downright immoral for private business to make any profit on government taxes at all. Perhaps, both practices should be eliminated but, what hypocrisy for Board opponents to point their fingers at this while ignoring or even profiting from it in the private sector.

Preferential Treatment

Another hue and cry often propigated by Liquor Board detractors involves the disparity of profit margins that are applied to Domestic versus Imported bands. Imported table wine is marked up in Ontario for example, well over 100% while Ontario table wines now only 37% . . . table wines from other provinces almost twice as much. Other provinces handle the matter similarly but with varying degrees of mark up.

On the surface such discrepancies appear to be callous examples of preferential treatment for domestic even provincial brands. Some even claim such practices contravene international trade agreements, GATT for example.

There is no possible way of circumventing this allegation. Liquor Boards are guilty as charged, of exercising preferential treatment. Yet, the Boards make no pretense really, at not extending local producers the long end of the stick. But by how much, really?

Although the disparity in such mark-ups makes it evident that preferential treatment towards local brands (by government directive) is official policy on the part of most Boards who have a provincial wine industry, the degree of advantage should not be equated with the obvious differences in mark-ups. Simply concluding, for example, that since some imported wine is jumped by 108% while local wine only 37%, therefore Niagara producers get a 71% advantage, would be misleading. For no such advantage exists when the bottom line is reached.

Domestic producers must warehouse and transport their products. Something quite foreign to local agents for Scotch or Beaujolais. They never actually handle the product. Agents of imported brands run essentially a **paper** type operation. So, when warehousing, transportation, money costs, personnel and a few other incidentals are thrown in, that 71% advantage could drop to 40% or less. This would be more realistic. Canadian winemakers are very much a part of a government 'don't step too hard on domestic toes' policy administered by their provincial Liquor Control Boards.

The Canadian public has made wine increasingly a part of our everyday life. The increasing role wine now plays in our society is indicative of the desire on the part of more and more people that vin ordinaires, everyday wines, be made available at more affordable prices.

Boards could buy such ordinary wines from a number of world producers, bottle them here, and make them available at very reasonable prices. In most provinces they don't. Quebec province being one major exception. And those that don't aren't likely to in the future. Why? Quite simply, the Canadian wine industry, growers and vintners alike, could not withstand that kind of competition. The results would mean that the pressures to transform the Niagara vineyard district into an asphalt parking lot and plant over Okanagan vineyards with apples would have increasing chances of success. Growers could be forced to sell or use their land for more profitable ventures. Even to the most casual observer, it's obvious that certain Liquor Boards are not about to initiate such a set of events. In fact new legislation has opened the door for Ontario wineries to import more fresh grapes, concentrates and bulk wines; even blending them with the local wines is no longer forbidden.

Price Comparison

But how do the two systems compare price-wise when they meet nose-to-nose over exactly the same legitimate label? As far as consumer 'beefs' go, this has been one we could label 'well done'. Buying a bottle of wine in a Toronto LCBO outlet, only to discover it goes for about 30% less at Joe's Liquor Store in Buffalo has, over the years, done little to win fans for the control system.

But why could a private New York or Washington State liquor and wine merchant sell an identical brand for less than economic giants the size of the Ontario, B.C. or Quebec Liquor Board? At least three added reasons, other than exorbitant mark-ups, have become evident: 'BARGAIN' BUYING, SMALL LOT PURCHASES, and FUTURES. Flexibility, more characteristic of private retailers, has made it possible for them to take advantage of the ups and downs of the world winemarket.

When the grapes are harvested and the wine is bottled, there simply isn't anymore of that vintage to be had. Because wine can improve with bottle ageing (spirits do not), and because the supply of better quality wine is fixed (by the size of the harvest), the entrepreneur and speculator find considerably more latitude in the wine trade to ply their skills.

This necessarily affects wine prices. They do fluctuate with demand. And admittedly it is also a manipulated commodity, prices frequently going much above a reasonable value. For decades this has favoured the more plyable nature of private enterprise.

Bargain Buying

As already established, **bargains** are easy to come by in the wine trade. That's all some producers have for sale · **bargains**. By being able to muzzle their integrity whenever convenient, some private wine merchants are able to display reputable looking labels at prices our Liquor Boards can only dream about. The English-Spanish-French bottle of St. Emilion spoken of earlier sold for less than $3.00 in England. In Vancouver, Toronto or Montreal an authentic Margaux fetches around $5.00. The difference in price . . . authenticity. In a N.Y. liquor store a 1973 Liebfraumilch (Qualitaetswein) was selling at $1.49. This merchant bought it from a U.S. wholesaler who in turn got it from an importer who in turn got it from a German shipper who bought it from a German producer. Either all in the chain had mysteriously turned benevolent with the public or this German Liebfraumilch came from Dunkirk. As unjust as it might seem this is the very nature of some of the comparisons used to chide Board pricing policies.

In all fairness though, authentic wine bargains do occasionally come to light. And private merchants with good trade contacts and a keen nose for a buy were always the ones to get them. The British wine trade is unexcelled at this. They have centuries of practice as well as numerous family ties to the vineyard areas themselves. The only problem with these legitimate bargains is lack of consistency. One week you might happen upon a deal, but don't expect to return next week for another bottle or to ever find it on a competitor's shelf. You have to be prepared and willing to live with their 'one shot' nature.

Bureaucratic bulk largely prohibited Liquor Boards from taking advantage of these occasional bargains, in the past. Each of their products had to be available in respectable quantities and at a price that was the same in Prince George as it was in Vancouver. There was really little provision in the 'control' system for bargain hunting. However in the past few years some provinces, notably Ontario and Quebec have established new divisions which deal with rare and special brands. They are quite energetic at procuring special allotments, small shipments and bargains - all passed on to the consumer, of course.

Small Lot Buying

Age, overstock, business failures, tight money, select labels of unique and rare character . . . are just some of the factors which at any time could make a small lot of very legitimate wine available. They were, in a sense, the exclusive territory of private merchants for generations. These special divisions of the Liquor Boards have changed this, though. No longer fettered by the requirements of large quantities needed to stock a number of outlets, these Boards can now ply the wine trade in a much broader fashion. With awesome purchasing power and impeccable commercial credentials, some Boards are now the match of any world wine buyer.

Wine Futures

From the moment of the grape harvest the future of that particular vintage comes under increasing attention and scrutiny. What will it be like? A great year? Will it be ordinary? What price will it demand? When will it mature?

Those interested in wine futures (early buying of wines that age well and will appreciate significantly in value) are constantly evaluating such ponderables. They anxiously await the producers' first announcement of the prices this vintage will draw.

Vintners or shippers may be able to determine the relative quality of the vintage as early as the Spring following the fermentation. Negotiations may start then. Or, they may find it to their advantage to wait until the vintage is ageing in cask or even bottled (some 2 years later) before announcing their individual prices. There are many eager clients waiting. For if they buy wisely their investment could return many times the original price in a few short years.

Among the more noteworthy clients keenly watching each vintage are now our Liquor Boards. Increasingly, since the middle sixties they less frequently allow these superior vintages to slip through their 'purchasing' hands. Board buyers are not uncommon figures in many of the world's vineyards at harvest time.

It's no longer rare to see two different vintages of the same wine sitting side by side in some of the larger liquor outlets. But when the Board buys futures there is a considerably different series of events that follow. And their long denounced excessive mark-ups make an about face.

The purpose of buying a wine future is to buy early and low, hold, and sell high. The independent wine merchant may buy a certain Chateau Bordeaux for $3.00 a bottle and six years later sell it for $30.00. Or, buy at $9.00 and sell at $100.00, in the same span. But when Boards buy early, they usually sell early.

Rather than see how long the price will keep growing, to sell only at the most profitable moment, the Board is still tied to its standard mark-up. While private merchants may in the end make 1000 or more percent, in relation to their purchase price, the Board is 'hoisted on its own pitard' so to speak. It usually cannot alter its established profit margins. So, since there is no advantage in holding a superior vintage; they become publicly available shortly after the vintage arrives. As a result, you have, in a personal way, the opportunity to buy your own wine futures, by buying early from the Board. You can even buy single bottles if you want. I recently opened a 1966 Chateau Langoa Barton, bought from a Board in 1969 for $4.30. In New York it sells for $18-$22 today. It works both ways though. A Chateau Latour listed by one Board at $60.00 can be had at $19.95 in Buffalo.

We must be cautious not to create an erroneous impression when discussing wine futures. 'Future' buying really only applies to the truly fine and great wines of the world. Fully 90% or more of the global vintage each year is of very ordinary nature. It has little 'future' - for it will, in all probability, be totally consumed by its third birthday. Of the 10% balance, half or less will be the subject of speculation.

But not all is profit with wine futures. It's always a gamble. Safer than most, but nonetheless a gamble. At some point the wine begins to decline in quality and saleability. At times speculators hold their stocks too long, only to discover the bottom has fallen out for that vintage. They may have overbought, money may be tight in general, or whatever, the consumer is just not buying at those prices. With warehousing and money costs the merchant may be happy to break even, on occasion.

A similar situation exists in the United States today. Many U.S. wine merchants seriously overbought numerous fine and great wines. In the last 10-12 years a glut of famed labels was brought into American stocks.

As many of these great wines were to hit their quality pinnacle in the early and mid 70's, wine merchants held them hoping to sell at peak prices. The economic slump of the seventies was not foreseen, and it evaporated much of the market for these high-priced wines. In an attempt to recover and release some of their long occupied, invested capital, consistent dumping has been evident in the last few years. To the point where unbelievable prices, as low as 50% of the price the producer is still asking, are not uncommon.

Although certainly as undesirable as this is for U.S. merchants, it is an ideal time for the American wine lover to add or build an enviable private wine cellar. The situation should not last longer than another 2 or 3 years, when more sane purchasing practices in recent years start to reach the consumer level.

Some private merchants are not quite so venturesome of spirit. They may buy early, say 1,000 cases of certain fine wines. Immediately they may sell 250 cases at a normal mark-up of anywhere from 30-75%. Two years later another 250 cases are put out for sale at perhaps 150-200% profit. A third 250 cases may appear in three more years time at possibly 400-500% profit. The last lot of 250 cases would hopefully go to market at the most auspicious moment, realizing 1000 or more percent profit. The wine would be eight years of age nearing its peak of quality.

Such an example is very general. Infinite shadings of buying, selling, time and quantities make this virtually an art form. Again, keep in mind such practices only take place with a very small percentage of each year's harvest. And depending on who bought what, when and where, Board, or private prices may show significant advantage for certain labels.

Comparisons of these two very different systems of distribution will continue as long as the two systems exist side by side. Opinions about them will remain diverse and vocal. Yet, despite real weaknesses a 'control' system works best. Its failings are evident but they continue to be the better of two evils.

In an age where freedom more often means the freedom to be victimized, the tighter, more structured approach of Liquor Boards have many attractions for the consumer. Its built-in safeguards provide a security, most often lacking in other systems. It's not the best or most ideal - it's just better.

Epilogue

There really isn't a foreseeable epilogue for wine. It's been with man almost from the beginning · a trusted balm, a beverage of joy. And perhaps it will be with us for an eternity of time to come. What more could be said for it.

How facetious it would be for anyone to consider that more than a scrap of wine knowledge could be contained on these few pages. It's been a reward to have been able to commit even this much to print. It hardly seemed like work though · for labour it was not.

To one of the grandest material blessings of a loving Creator · may we all treat WINE with the respect and moderation it deserves.

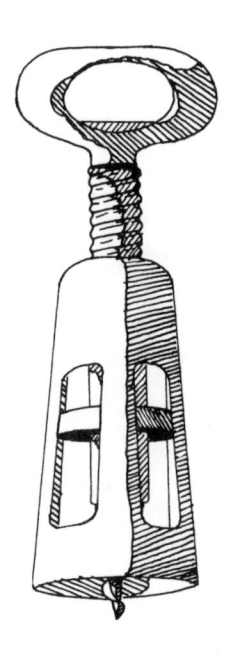

Index

Absinthium, 157
abstainer, 39, 83
acetic acid, 80, 181
acid, 21, 25, 41. 79, 80, 96, 110
Adams, Porter, 32, 99
after taste, 79
age, 49, 50, 52, 57, 64, 107, 110, 139, 140, 142, 159, 165, 186
agitation, 163
alcohol, 19, 20, 35, 47, 49, 76, 77, 92, 94, 97, 106-108, 133, 145, 149, 150, 155, 159
Alfold, 150
Algeria, 117, 179
Aloes, 157
Alsace, 78, 84, 110, 143
amber, 62, 160, 161
amontillado, 160, 162
anaesthetic, 96
Andulucian, 160
Anjou, 83, 84, 149, 179
anthocynin, 96
antibiotic, 96
Antoinette, Marie, 158
anti-wine snob, 13-16
A.O.C., 116, 117
aperitif, 157
Appellation Contrôlée, 115, 117, 180
Armagnac, 167
aroma, 21, 24, 27, 43, 72, 77, 100, 125, 150, 157, 160
Artemisia Absinthium, 157
arteriosclerosis, 93
asbestos, 59
Assyria, 19
Asti Spumonte, 131
astringent, 68
Atlantic, 18, 43, 160
auslese, 147, 148
Australia, 154, 162
Austria, 62, 154, 155
Avignon, 123
Avize, 129

Baby Duck, 106, 108
Baby Duckling, 106
Babylon, 19
Baco, Maurice, 110
Baco Noir, 109, 110
bacteria, 47, 96
Baden, 146, 155
bain-marie, 139
balanced, 27, 78-80
Barbera, 142
Bardolino, 88, 89, 137
Barnee, 108
Barolo, 79, 83, 137, 141, 142
barrel, 50, 52, 117, 161
basement-buff, 19, 54
Beaujolais, 16, 49, 53, 77, 79, 100, 110-112, 123, 127, 176, 185
Beaujolais Superieure, 127
Beaujolais Villages, 127
Beaune, 123
beechwood, 59
beef, 82
beer, 33, 40, 59, 180
beerenauslese, 147
bentonite, 59
Bible, 48
Black Canaiolo, 140
Black Forest, 145
Black Tower, 56
Blanc de Blanc, 129
Blanc de Noir, 129
blending, 27, 56-58, 135, 161, 165, 178
bleu cheese, 83
blood, 58, 88
blueberry, 19, 20, 54
Bodensee, 143
body, 21, 78, 79, 129, 167
Bouchard, Paul, 126
Bordeaux, 49, 52-54, 56, 61, 62, 83, 93, 117-119, 121, 122, 167, 177, 179, 180, 189
bottle, 40, 43, 53, 140, 141, 144, 145
bottling, 114, 138

Index

bouquet, 21, 27, 53, 68, 72, 77, 79, 122, 127, 144, 147, 149, 160, 162, 167
brand, 56, 88, 173, 175, 176
Brandy, 21, 38, 159, 163-165
bread, 88, 91, 92
breed, 135
Breisgau, 143
brick-red, 62
Brie, 83
British Columbia, 27, 35, 84, 186
Brolio, 141
Brouilly, 127
brown, 62, 64
Bual, 158
bubbles, 59-61
Burgundy, 49, 52-54, 56, 62, 78, 79, 83, 96, 112, 118, 121, 123, 125, 127, 128
Cabernet, 119, 120, 122
Cabernet Franc, 119
Cabernet Sauvignon, 57, 119
California, 26, 54, 55, 84, 93, 96, 114, 115, 120, 130, 150-152, 162
calories, 96-98
Camembert, 83
Camomile, 157
canapes, 84
Canada Duck, 106, 108
cane-sugar, 25, 94, 159
caps, 43, 52, 94, 147
carbohydrate, 97
carbon dioxide, 19, 47, 61, 74, 100, 102
carbonic maseration, 100, 112
cardomon, 157
caramel, 138
carrots, 19, 54
cask, 50, 52, 138, 140, 141, 156, 162, 163
Catawba, 151
Cazapra, 158
cellar, 122
Chablis, 56, 79, 84, 85, 110, 111, 123, 125

Chalonnaise, 123
Chambertin, 123, 128
Champagne, 56, 59, 79, 82, 85, 108, 110, 112, 114, 129, 130-132, 165
chaptalization, 25, 26
character, 49, 50, 101, 110, 133, 162
Chardonnay, 27, 57, 110, 111, 125, 126
Charente, 162
charmat, 59
Charmes, 128
Chase, Emily, 97
chateau, 93, 113, 115, 116, 119, 121, 188
Chateau Ausone, 120
Chateau Carbonnieux, 122
Chateau Chalon, 162
Chateau Figeac, 120
Chateau Haut-Bailly, 122
Chateau Haut Brion, 121
Chateau Lafite, 120, 122, 123
Chateau, Margaux, 15, 120
Chateauneuf-du-Pape, 79, 131, 133
Chateau Pavie, 120
Chateau, Talbot, 119
cheddar, 53
cheese, 82, 160
Chelois, 29, 109, 110
chemical, 20, 40, 100
Chenas, 127
cherries, 54
chestnut, 52
Cheval Blanc, 120
Chianti, 56, 88, 139-141, 177
chicken, 88-90
Chile 153
chill, 91
Chiroubles, 127
cholesterol, 93, 97
chowder, 85
Churchill, Winston, 158
Cincinnati, 151
Cinsault, 133
Cinzano, 158
citric acid, 80

193

CIVB, 180
clams, 85
claret, 54, 63, 118, 119
clarity, 58, 63
classico, 140, 141
classification, 120-122
clay, 137
Cleveland, 151
climate, 28, 49, 78, 112
Clinton, 32
Clos de Beze, 128
cloudy, 58
Cognac, 21, 162, 165-168
Cold Duck, 108
Cold Duckling, 108
Cold Turkey, 106, 108
colic, 96
colitis, 96
colour, 38, 61, 72, 110, 133, 137, 138, 144, 147
Common Market, 117, 179
commune, 128
concentrates, 29, 55, 56, 185
Concord, 32, 37, 44, 100, 102, 107
connoisseur, 14, 16, 23, 137, 149
constipation, 96
control, 170, 171, 175, 177, 178, 180-182, 187, 190
Controllata, 134, 135
Controllata e garantita, 135
Cooksville, 32, 99
cooking, 85-87, 96, 159
Coq au Vin, 87-89
coquilles, 88
Corbieres, 117
cork, 53, 73, 74, 94, 179
corkscrew, 72, 74, 75, 180
Corsica, 117, 179
Costieres du Gard, 117
Cote-de-Brouilly, 127
Cote d'Or, 123, 128
Cote de Provence, 117
Cotes de Nuits, 123
Cotes du Luberon, 117
crackling, 82, 84, 149

cradle, 71, 140
Cream Sherry, 160, 161
crossbreed, 29, 108
cutting, 103
Czechoslovakia, 171

dandelion, 19, 54
D'Artagnan, 167
decant, 71
decanter, 8
de Chaunac, 29, 109, 110
Delaware, 32
Delaware, Lord, 31
Denominazione D'Origine, 134
dessert wine, 32, 44, 84, 138, 161
Diana, 32
diaphoretic, 96
diarrhea, 96
diet, 96, 97
distillation, 21, 162, 164, 167, 168, 181
diuretic, 96
doctors, 36, 93-95
Domaine de Chevallier, 122
dosed, 159
Drayton, Sir Henry, 41
dry, 20, 32, 38, 68, 68, 76, 82-85, 89, 94, 98, 121, 125, 126, 137, 138, 159, 160
dull, 68, 80
Dunkirk, 117, 179, 187

earthy, 110, 153
Edam, 83
egg, 85, 90, 91
Egri Bikaver, 106
Egypt, 19
Eiswein, 148
Elbling, 143
ellagic acid, 96
Emerald Riesling, 143
England, 67, 118, 173, 179, 180, 186
enologist — see oenologist
enzymes, 92
Erie, Lake, 151

Ericson, Leif, 7, 30
Est Est Est, 135, 137
estate bottled, 113, 115, 128
estufa, 159
evaporation, 34, 53
Exposition Universelle, 120

fabricated, 25
fermentation, 25, 49, 50, 54, 76, 112, 130, 140, 141, 156, 159, 162, 181, 188
fiaschi, 139, 141
filter, 59
filtration, 59
fine, 15, 21-23, 26, 64, 68, 115, 121, 145, 151, 154, 155
Finger Lakes, 151
fining, 58
Finland, 171
Fino, 159, 160, 162
fir, 156
fish, fresh water, 85
flask, 140
flat, 80
flavor, 25, 49, 79, 122, 156
Fleurie, 127
Flor, 162
flowery, 78, 145, 160
foche, 109
fortified, 138
foxy, 24, 32, 50, 100-102, 109, 110
fragrance, 78, 86, 167
Franc, 119

France, 13, 15, 17, 19, 27, 34, 53, 54, 84, 88, 93, 95, 102, 105, 112-120, 123, 125, 141, 144, 149, 158, 163, 179
free enterprise, 170
fruit, 20, 21, 54, 77, 82, 160
fruity, 27, 77, 127, 137, 147, 155
Fuddle Duck, 106
full, 78, 110, 127, 133, 158
futures, 106, 186, 188, 189

Gamay, 27, 57, 110-112, 127
gamma-butyrolactone, 96
gamma-hydroxybutyric, 96
Garda, Lake, 137
garlic, 88, 91, 98
Gascony, 118, 167
gastro-intestinal, 96
Gattinara, 141, 142
gelatin, 59
generic, 56, 111, 112
Germany, 17, 25, 26, 62, 78, 92, 131, 143-146, 148, 187
Gevrey-Chambertin, 128
Gewurtztraminer, 143, 155
Gironde, 119
glasses, 72, 73
glycerol, 92
gold, 62, 126
Golden Goose, 108
Gorganjola, 83
Gouda, 83
gormet, 98
governo, 140, 141
Grand Cru, 128
Gran Vino, 153
grape-growers, 36, 50
grapejuice, 20
grapelism, 17
Graves, 85, 121
Graves de Bordeaux, 121
Graves, Superieure, 121
great, 14, 15, 21-23, 68, 121, 125, 137
Greece, 155, 156
green, 62, 100, 145
greenish, 62
Grenache, 133
Grey Riesling, 143
Gumpoldskirchener, 155
Gutedel, 143

Havarti, 83
heart disease, 93
heavy, 78, 150

honey, 19, 54
hors d'oeuvre, 83, 84
Hot Goose, 106
Hungary, 106, 150
hybrids, 8, 27-29, 44, 102, 107, 109, 110, 151, 154

ice-water, 68
Icewine, 148
importer, 68, 173
imported, 8, 24, 27, 33, 34, 43, 100, 105, 106, 151, 180, 181
insomnia, 97
inter-cellular fermentation, 100
intestinal bacteria, 96
intestinal colic, 96
iron, 92
Isabella, 32
isinglass, 59
Italy, 13, 17, 34, 53, 62, 93, 105, 117, 134, 137, 140-142, 155, 158, 179

jacknife, 64
Jadot, Louis, 113
jam, 12, 35
jelly, 12, 35
Jerez, 160
Jesuit, 99
Johannisberg, 144
Jolly Friar, 108
Judge Frost, 108
Julienas, 127
Jurancon, 167

Kabinett, 147
Kadarka, 150, 151
Kaiserstuhl, 143, 146
Kerner, 143
Kuhlmann, 110

label, 14, 34, 56, 67, 72, 100, 105, 111, 115, 116, 118, 121, 134, 153, 155, 165, 175, 178, 179
label-drinker, 15

Labrusca, 24, 25, 27-29, 32, 44, 100, 107-110
lactic acid, 80
Languedoc, 54
Lichine, 106
Liebfraumilch, 117, 146, 147, 186, 187
light, 44, 68, 82, 83, 110, 118, 137, 155
Limousin, 52
Liquor Board, 9, 12, 34, 39-42, 56, 95, 106, 118, 145, 151, 153, 170-175, 177, 181, 183-185, 187, 188, 190
Liverpool, 138, 179
lobster, 85
Loire, 54, 84, 88, 129, 149
Longman's, 97
louse, 102
Lucia, Dr. S.P. 96
Luxembourg, 144

Maconnais, 123
Madeira, 61, 82, 85, 87, 138, 158, 159
Mainz, 147
Malbec, 119
mallic acid, 80
Malmsey, 158
Malvasia, 158
Manzanilla, 160
Marchio Nazionale, 134
Marechal Foch, 29, 109, 110
margarine, 98
Margaux, 120, 179, 186
marjoram, 98
Markgraflerland, 143
Marsala, 61, 87, 138, 139
martini, 157
Martini & Rossi, 158
Massachusetts, 95
Mateus, 106
mature, 48, 77
Mavrodaphne, 156
medicine, 92, 94

Index

Medoc, 119, 120, 122
Merlot, 119, 122
Mesnil, Le, 129
metallic, 125
methode champenoise, 59
methyl anthranilate, 100
Meursault, 123
micro-climate, 26
microorganism, 49, 50, 162
milk, 58, 78, 85, 92
minerals, 92, 97
Minervois, 117
mis en bouteille au Chateau, 113
mis en bouteille du Domaine, 115
Molinara, 137
Montefiascone, 135
Montrachet, 85, 110, 111, 123, 126
Morgon, 128
Morio-muscat, 143
Morocco, 117, 179
Moselle, 78, 84, 144, 145
Moulin-a-vent, 127
Mouton Cadet, 106
Muller-Thurgau, 143, 145, 146
Muscadet, 85, 88, 89
muscat, 85, 155, 158, 167
mushroom, 88-90, 98
Musketeers, 167
must, 148

Nahe, 146
Napoleon, 128, 165
Nebbiolo, 141
negociant, 113
Negrara, 137
Nelson, Lord, 138
New York, 106, 151, 186
Niagara, 36, 50, 107, 185
nice, 23
Nipozzano, 141
Noah, 48
noble, 22, 23, 50, 137, 145
Noilly-Prat, 158
no-no, 66
North America, 7, 18, 25, 30-32, 52, 67, 93, 94, 100, 102, 103, 110, 111, 149, 161

oak, 51, 163
oaky, 50
oenologist, 22, 48
Ohio, 151-153
Okanagan, 185
Oloroso, 159, 160
Ontario, 27, 29, 32, 35, 36, 39, 42, 99, 100, 106, 180, 184-187,
orange, 64
ordinary, 15, 21-23, 27, 28, 49, 55, 68, 79, 110, 113, 116, 121, 123, 150, 189,
organic acids, 92
Original Abfüllung, 115
Ortenau, 143
oxidation, 53, 64
oxygen, 102
oysters, 85

packaging, 107, 108
palatable, 22, 99, 150
palate, 137
Palatinate, 146
Paris, 120
parsley, 85, 91, 98
Pasteur, Louis, 92
Pauillac, 120
perch, 85
Persia, 19
Petit Chablis, 125
Petit Verdot, 119, 122
phylloxera, 102
Picpoul, 167
Piedmont, 141, 142
pigment, 96
pink, 64
Pinot, 111, 127
Pinot Blanc, 111
Pinot Noir, 27, 57, 106, 110, 111, 153
pipette, 167
pizza 139
Pontet Canet, 120
poor, 15, 21-23, 116
pop-wine, 61, 107, 108
pork, 82
Port, 49, 56, 61, 94, 98, 138, 159, 160

Portugal, 150, 160
Portugeiser, 143
pot-still, 163
Pouilly Fuisse, 84, 85, 110, 123
Pouilly Fume, 85
poultry, 82
Prefontaine, 56
preservative, 25, 107
Prohibition, 34-39, 94, 151
proprietaire, 113
protein, 92, 97
Provence, 129, 141
Puglia, 117, 179
Puligny-Montrachet, 126
pungent, 43
purple, 62

Qualitatswein, 26, 146, 186
Qualitatswein mit Pradikat, 26, 147
Quebec, 31, 106, 185-187

Redwood, 52
refrigerator, 37, 65, 68, 91, 97
region, 50, 123, 140, 145, 151
Reservado, 153
Retsina, 155
Rheingau, 144, 146, 147
Rheinhessen, 146
Rhine River 145
Rhode Island, 32
Rhone, 54, 83, 141, 149
Riesling, 27, 57, 78, 83, 84, 85, 90, 143-146, 153, 155
Riparia, 110
Riserva Ducale, 106, 141
Rome, 19, 135, 136
Rondinella, 137
rootstock, 103
Roquefort, 83
rosé, 68, 82, 83, 85, 98, 117, 149 150, 179
Rothchild (see Chateau Lafite)
Rulander, 143
Rupestris, 110
Ruwer, 144
Rye, 12, 14, 28, 177

Saar, 144
Saint Emilion, 119, 180, 186
salad, 77, 98, 160
saltwater fish, 85
Samos, 156
Sangiovese, 140
Santiago, 153
Saumur, 84
Sauterne, 61, 120
Sauvignon, 120
Sauvignon Blanc, 121
scallops, 88, 89
Scheurebe, 143
Schiller, Johann, 32, 99
Schloss, 147
Schloss Johannisberg - see Johannisberg
Scotch, 28, 185
seafood, 82, 84, 160
second fermentation, 40, 59, 60, 140
sediment, 40, 60, 71
Seibel, 109, 110
Sekt, 131
Semillion, 121
Semplice, 134
senility, 64
Sercial, 158
Sete, 117, 179
Sherry, 12, 25, 56, 61, 82, 85, 87, 94, 97, 138, 159, 161, 162
shipper, 113, 115, 163
shrimps, 90, 91
Sicily, 117, 138, 179
slate, 144
slip-skin, 24
Smith, Capt. John, 30, 31
smoked, 85
Sno Bird, 107
Soave, 89
soda pop, 59, 105, 107
Soil, 49, 78, 112, 121, 133, 137, 167
solera, 138, 161
soup, 82, 160
South Africa, 162
South America, 120
Spain, 117, 118, 159, 160-162, 179
sparkling, 68, 108

Index

sparkloids, 59
Spatburgunder, 143
spatlese, 147, 155
species, 24, 26, 100
St. Amour, 127
staphylococcus, 96
steak, 61
St. Emilion, 120, 167
St. Julien, 120
storage, 65
straw, 62, 121, 125, 139
strawberry, 81, 91
sugar, 19, 20, 25, 26, 40, 43, 49, 54, 76, 77, 91, 92, 159
sugar content, 25, 26
sweet, 20, 61, 76, 82, 94, 96, 138, 148, 149, 159, 160
swiss cheese, 83
Sylvaner, 143, 145, 146, 155
syrup, 138, 148
Szekszardi, Voros, 150, 151

table wine, 68, 93, 109, 141, 143
Tafelwein, 26
tanks, 59, 117, 130, 178
tannins, 119
tart, 25, 80, 125
tastevin, 62
tasting, 68, 176
Tavel, 149
Tennessee White Oak, 52
Temperance, 35, 36, 41, 94
temperature, 38, 65-68, 161
thyme, 98
Tilsit, 83
Traminer, 83-85
tranquilizer, 96
Trebbiano, 140
trockenbeerenauslese, 147
Trollinger, 143
trout, 85
tulip-shape, 72
turpentine, 156
Turin 158
Tuscany, 140
Tyrol, 155

United Farmers' Party, 35, 38
United States, 26, 102, 105-107, 118, 151, 171, 173, 175, 179, 187, 189, 190

Valpolicello, 88, 89, 137
varietal, 54, 56, 57, 109, 111, 112, 153, 155
vascular, 93
vastatrix - see phylloxera
V.C.C., 116
V.D.Q.S., 116
Veeburg, 29, 109
vegetable, 20, 21
Veltliner, 155
velvety, 137
vendange, 154
Vendemmia, 134
Verdelet, 29, 109
Verdelho, 158
vermouth, 157, 158
Verona, 137
vibration, 66
Villa Antinori, 141
Villard Noir, 29
vin aigre, 80
vinegar, 40, 41, 80, 84, 181
vineyard, 21, 26, 36, 50, 102, 103, 109, 112, 113, 115, 126, 138, 145, 147, 160
Vinifera, Vitis, 25-28, 43, 44, 109, 110
Vineland, 7, 30, 100
Vin Mousseux, 131
vintage, 21, 49, 57, 103, 123, 132, 146, 147, 150, 151, 161, 186, 188, 189
vintner, 111, 141
Virginia, 30
vitamins, 92, 97
viticulture, 146, 153
Vitis, 24, 100
volatile acid, 40, 41, 181
V.S. 165
V.S.O.P., 165

199

water, 25, 37, 38, 41, 54, 76, 78
Wermut, 157
whiskey, 21, 28, 33, 38
wine, 18, 19, 21, 47, 48
winemaker, 41, 100, 102, 111
winery, 36, 37, 41, 42, 58
wine-snob, 13, 14, 16
wing-style, 64
Winnipeg, 144
wonder-drug, 95, 96
woody, 50
Worcestershire, 89, 98
wormwood, 157

Xerex, 160

yeast, 19, 47, 49, 50, 54, 76, 92, 162
yield, 38, 123

Zabaglione, 138
Zinfandel, 150

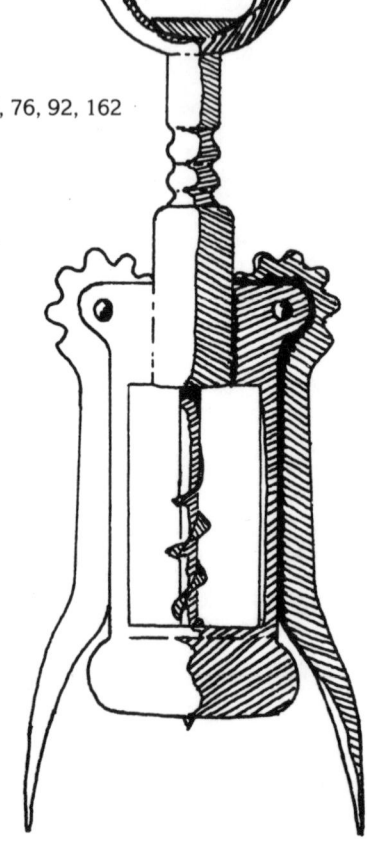